The Marks of the Nails

By Paul Urbano

Published by:
Yellow Bird Division
Economic Information, Inc.
Box 5127
St. Paul, Minnesota 55104

Economic Information, Inc.
Yellow Bird Division
Box 5127
St. Paul, Minnesota 55104

"The Monk of the Silver Bell" reprinted with permission from the *Arizona Republic,* where the story first appeared in one of a series of columns entitled "Orthodox" by the author.

Cover and inside illustrations by Mary De Loyht of Phoenix, Arizona.

$3.50

International Standard Book Number 0-913514-04-7.
Library of Congress Catalog Card Number 73-90039.

PRINTED IN THE UNITED STATES OF AMERICA.

To my wife
Carol

CONTENTS

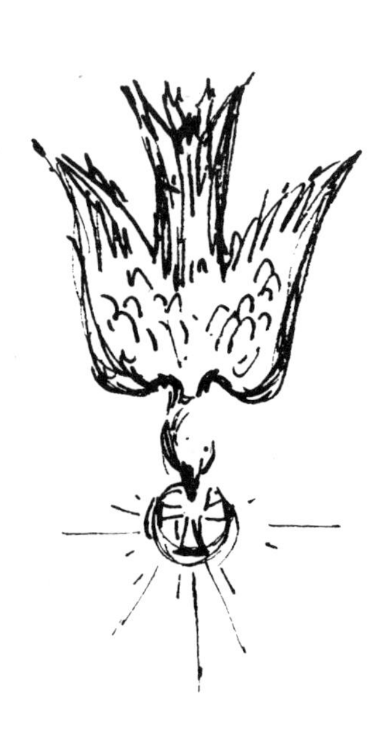

FOREWORD

Little as some of them may look it, all these pieces were done as working sermons, for use in the pulpit – not as writings. But since I speak and write pretty much the same, I have not changed them except to take out an occasional "today" or "all of us in this building."

What concerns me much more than their style is the fact that, because they were written to convey the gospel to a congregation, not for publication, I kept no record of my indebtedness to other men. In addition, I have the kind of mind which retains with great exactness what I have read, and must certainly have reproduced here many sentences just as other men set them down. I am especially indebted (obviously) to William James, Gerald Kennedy and Leslie Weatherhead, not so obviously to Frederick Robertson and others of the great. But at least I can hope that what I have lifted is mostly in the public domain. And I take some comfort from a saying of the late beloved Bishop of Arizona, Arthur Kinsolving, that "there is no plagiarism in preaching." We preach to proclaim the Gospel, and cannot expect, in such an ancient calling, to be altogether original.

Paul D. Urbano
Phoenix, Arizona
July 31, 1973

The Centurion

"Now the centurion and they that were with him watching Jesus, when they saw the earthquake and the things that were done, feared exceedingly saying, Truly this was the Son of God."

St. Matthew 27:54

I am called Gaius Marcus, of the gens Julius (a family distinguished for military service to the state and, in fact, the family from which came the first real Caesar). I am Centurion of the Augustan Cohort of the auxiliaries stationed in Palestine.

This cohort, a unit from Sebaste which achieved some glory a few years ago by putting down a Zealot insurrection, has been rewarded with the special honor of being permitted to name itself "Augustan" and to carry in its colors a special medallion with the emperor's image. But it is not Roman. It cannot even speak Latin. It speaks Greek, and bad Greek at that. And I, purely Roman, was attached to it as a punishment. Two years ago on the Rhine Frontier, while commanding a cohort of true Romans, I led my men too far pursuing the Germans into their dark forests, and fell into an ambush, and lost too many legionaries. And so the vengeful old Tiberius sent me here to sweat in stinking Jerusalem.

So be it. I have endured punishment before. This is my twenty-second year of service under the eagles of Rome; and I have endured much. My whole life from young manhood on has been lived to the sound of the iron-soled boots of the legions pounding over the Roman roads to the four corners of the world. And I have seen much. But by two-faced Janus, Keeper of the Door of Life, never anything like what I have seen in this city of the Jews.

Less than two weeks ago it all began, a little before the festival the Jews call Passover. The Jews have a myth stating that under their greatest commander,[1] one Moses, they, who had been slaves of the Egyptians, contrived to escape into the Negeb, the wilderness around the Mountain of the Moon,[2] because the chariots of the Egyptians stuck in the mud of the Sea of Reeds.[3] And they celebrate this deliverance at Passover.

[1]Whereas we think of Moses as a prophet, he was also in fact a commander, and would appear to be entirely that to a Roman.

[2]The ancient name for Sinai.

[3]A common ancient name for the section that the Bible calls "The Red Sea."

Well, it may be so. The Egyptians were never very much in the field, even at their best. They relied on sheer numbers and were not even properly armed. And I have no use for cavalry in any form, anyway. Cavalry has never yet broken the Roman line.[4] What one needs in war is tough, disciplined infantry, carrying man-sized shields and skilled in the use of javelin and shortsword. We hurl our javelins like a shower of death at thirty paces and then close with the shortsword, and nothing in the world can withstand us. But these are things that all the world knows.

From what I have seen of these Jews, they are not exactly milk drinkers, either, and might give some trouble to any but regular Roman troops. Some of them, nick-named "Sicarii" after their daggers – they are also called "Zealots" – habitually carry long knives under their cloaks and murder us at every opportunity. And if a dispute arises over their religion, the Jews act as if their whole city were being burned to the ground.

Take, for example, the dispute over our "iconic" standards. As befits a cohort named "Augustan," our standards have the image of the princeps on them, the image of Augustus Caesar. And as befits two good Romans, another centurion and I burned incense before these images the morning after arriving in Jerusalem from Caesarea. And right away, Pilate, the prefect, was beseiged by a howling mob, screaming that this was contrary to their law, throwing dust on their heads like roosters on a

[4]The Roman line never was broken until Gothic cavalry accomplished it at the Battle of Adrianople. But by that time there was hardly a native Roman in the Roman army.

dunghill, tearing their clothes, and risking their very lives by mobbing the sentries.[5]

But that was nothing. When, later on, Pilate, in the best Roman tradition, arranged to build an aqueduct for Jerusalem, he naturally took some of the money for it out of the temple treasury. After all, was the aqueduct not for the Jews? Why should they not contribute? But, no. This was, according to the Jews, a desecration of sacrificial gifts. And first they spat in the water; then they broke the aqueduct; and finally they walked all the way to Caesarea where Pilate was in residence, collecting many more fanatics on the road, and confronted the prefect with fierce impudence. Before this incident was over, the main square of Caesarea literally ran with Jewish blood.[6]

I tell you, they are wilder and more determined than even the Britons, and must be seen to be believed. But I, of course, am accustomed to barbarians of every kind. They are usually more a nuisance than anything else. They disturb the peace of the empire and have to be put down without mercy. All that is perfectly natural. It is the way of the world.

But what has lately happened to me in this city is not natural. Neither is it the way of the world. Whatever it means (and I am not sure about that), it is not natural.

I refer to the events which, as I said, began a little before Passover.

---

[5]The substance of this incident is reported by Josephus in the **Antiquities** and **Wars.**

[6]So substantially Josephus in **Wars.**

This . . . what shall I call him? This "Man"? I think he was not a man. Yet he seemed perfectly to be one. He acted in some ways like a god. But a strange kind of god. He was *kind.* Who ever heard of a kind god? It is the nature of gods to be indifferent to men unless they want something. And then, he could not have been a god because we were able to kill him. Yet . . . Well, you see, I am perplexed about this.

But let me tell you from the beginning what happened.

The Jews[7] were highly incensed against this Jesus bar Joseph[8] because, they said, he was guilty of blasphemy for making himself equal with God. This was, on the face of it, a ridiculous charge. For as everyone knows, there are many gods, and no man can make himself the equal of any one of them. To them, we are nothing. They kill us for their sport.

But in any case, blasphemy, under the law of the Jews, carries the death penalty. And since the Jews cannot put anyone to death without our consent (and, indeed, not without our carrying out the execution for them), they first condemned this Jesus bar Joseph in their high court,

---

[7]The writer's credentials as a friend of the Jewish people are incontestable. (See also comments on p. 73: "But have not the Jews suffered enough? . . .) He is also aware that the anti-Semitism of the gospels reflects the sub-apostolic age, when the young Christian community was, in fact, suffering from Jewish persecution. Such persecution is entirely understandable to anyone who knows the situation of the Jews at the time. Moreover, modern Jews are no more responsible for the actions of their ancestors than this writer is obligated to pay "reparations" to the authors of the Black Manifesto. But I do not see the necessity of expressing friendliness for the Jews by expunging the whole gospel record of their unfriendliness to Jesus, as is sometimes done now.

[8]A first-century Jew would have one name of his own, plus "son of" (bar), plus his father's name. Thus, to the world at large, Jesus would be "bar Joseph."

called the Great Sanhedrin, and then dragged him before Pilate for official sentencing.

Pilate, of course, was at first bored by the whole business. He looks with contempt upon the endless religious controversies of the Jews. More than that, he had had too much wine the night before – as usual – and was rumored to have been quarreling with his wife.

He snarled at everybody as he came up onto the so-called "Pavement" where he sits to judge. When the sentries let the Jews in and they all began screaming at once the way they do, I thought for a moment that Pilate would order the troops to exterminate the lot of them. As I have told you, he has done that sort of thing before. He put his hands over his head and grew pale with rage.

But since the Caesarea affair and the trouble over the Augustan icons, Pilate has not been in good odor with Tiberius and he did not want another bloody riot reported to the Emperor. He did go so far as to have the maniple of soldiers on duty level their spears and walk slowly into the crowd. That quieted them down at least enough so that one could hear. The chief men of the Jews made their accusations and demanded death for the prisoner. Then they brought the prisoner in . . .

For some reason, it was suddenly – and utterly – quiet. It was much like the quietness just before a storm breaks in nature. One feels in such a quiet that enormous forces are about to break loose.

I looked at Pilate from where I stood beside his curial chair, and what I saw upon his face was perplexity and uneasiness. It might even have been fear. Fear of what? I do not know. Perhaps fear of the unknown.

The prisoner stood about five feet and ten inches (the average Roman is six inches less[9]), and was made like a first-class legionary. Though he must have been more than thirty years old, he showed no signs of aging, and there was not an ounce of fat on him. He was clean-shaven in the Roman manner and had his hair clipped like ours, too.[10] He stood there before Pilate and said nothing. And by all the gods, he was beautiful with a beauty that was all within. It was as if everything that goes into the making of a proper man had been poured into him – everything.

We stood and looked at him. And then Pilate said, "Ecce homo!" – "Behold the man!"

I know why he said it. We were all thinking it. And, of course, in the Latin tongue "ecce homo" could mean just as well "Behold *man*" or "Look at what a man should be."

Pilate shook himself a little as if coming out of a daze and began to question the prisoner: "Have you heard the accusations against you?"

The prisoner nodded once, slowly.

"What say you to these charges? Are you, in fact, some kind of king?"

Here the answer was cryptic: "You are the one who says so."

---

[9]The Romans were small – and tough. An American of average stature can hardly fit himself into the stone seats that are left in the Roman ruins.

[10]Jesus was brought up in Galilee near "The Decapolis", ten cities largely Gentile in custom. And (peace to Sallman and too many other artists, peace also to the hippies who suppose they "look like Jesus"); the only extant likeness which may be his appears on the Chalice of Antioch, where he is pictured as here.

I was startled. I know that Pilate was startled, too. One does not speak impudently to a Roman prefect sitting as magistrate, who is not only a judge but a commander who can order his troops to carry out his sentence. But then, watching the prisoner's face, we saw that it was not his intention to be impudent. He was merely speaking in that cryptic style which is natural to the Eastern mind.

Pilate continued, "Is that all you have to say to me? Do you not realize who I am, and that I have power to crucify you and power to let you go? I think you had better speak more plainly to me. Are you some kind of king?"

The prisoner said, "Sir, my kingdom is not of this world."

"Of *what* world, then?" asked the prefect.[11] "Is there more than one world? And does not Rome hold all of this one?"

"There is another world," said the prisoner, quite simply. He sounded not only as if he believed it, but as if he wanted to open some kind of door and invite us into that other world.

"I begin to understand what this business is," Pilate said. "You are guilty of nothing more than madness. Yet," he continued, "you do not have the look of *madness* about you. Is this, perhaps, an altercation over one of your Jewish superstitions? If it is, I will throw it out of my court."

---

[11]The reader will have noticed that "Prefect" is used throughout instead of "Procurator." The ascription of the title "Procurator" to Pilate appears to be based upon an anachronism in Josephus (Wars). During the reigns of Augustus and Tiberius, governors of Judea were called "prefects."

"It is no superstition. There is another world."

"And in that other world you are a king?"

"You say that I am."

Pilate threw up his hands. "Water!" When the water was brought, he washed his hands before the crowd, saying, "I wash my hands of this affair. I cannot see that this man is worthy of death. He has done nothing against Caesar. It is all some question of religious opinion; and one religious opinion is as good as another."

Then the Jews began to scream, "We have a law, and according to our law he deserves to die! Crucify him!"

Pilate averted his eyes from the prisoner's face. No doubt he was thinking of the debauched and cruel old man on the Island of Capri who was every day more suspicious of everybody and more fearful of violence, and who would doubtless remove Pilate if violence erupted in Judea.

"Very well," Pilate said at last in a low, troubled voice. "Let him be crucified."

It is customary, as everyone knows, to flog a man before crucifying him. In fact, except when large numbers are being crucified all at once, it is mandatory – and something of a mercy, because after being cut to pieces by the Roman flagellum, which is made of strips of leather with bits of lead and sharp bone embedded in them, the poor wretch does not last so long on the cross.

But that is the only mercy in this miserable death we have inherited from our ancient enemies, the Carthaginians. And a strong man will often last for two or three days even after flogging. I remember one pirate who lasted a week.

A bad way to die, this. After a time, the man finds he can inhale but cannot exhale – because of the position of his arms. Then all his muscles go into spasm, as sometimes also happens when a man dies of a poisoned wound and his jaws lock shut.[12] Only in these two cases have I seen such spasms. I thank the gods that I am a Roman citizen and can never be crucified.

Well, never mind that now. I used to take great comfort from my conviction that, after death, there is nothing. I had even determined upon my epitaph, borrowed from the Greeks: "I was not; I was; I am not; I care not."[13] Now I am not so sure . . .

We took the prisoner into the barracks of the Antonia Fortress and stripped him, and proceeded with the flogging. The flogging went badly. The men were nervous for some reason; and after he was bound to the post, the prisoner stood with his chin raised and his eyes shut – as if he had withdrawn himself somehow from his body – and never uttered a sound. The men took turns with the lash as usual, but nobody delivered more than two or three strokes before he handed the flagellum to another and went to the wine barrel. By the time we finished, the men were half drunk.

Suddenly, despite his great dignity and endurance, we began to *mock* the prisoner. I know why we mocked him. It was an attempt to cut down his size so that we could endure what we were doing to him.

---

[12]Tetanus.

[13]An actual Greek epitaph uncovered at Rome, dating from near the first century.

We made a crown of the thorn bush called "tribolos," on which the goats and camels feed in this strange land, and stuck it on his head, making his head bleed copiously; and we put a papyrus reed in his hand for a sceptre, and gave him an old purple blanket to cover him, and bent the knee and said, "Hail, King!" And we took turns slapping his face and saying, "Prophesy, Prophet. Who slapped you?"

But it was all quite dismal, and not as lively as it sounds. In truth, some of my hardened men vomited in their disgust and had to drink more wine. And all this time the prisoner never said a word.

It is about two miles from the Tower Antonia to the hill called "Place of a Skull" where we crucify criminals, Jerusalem being, by Roman standards, not a big city; it accommodates its huge population by piling people one on top of each other like ants. Indeed, yes; Jerusalem is like a great stone anthill. And these Jews enjoy being crowded together in a way which would drive even a Roman plebeian from the Trans-Tiber out of his wits. And they are like certain animals that live in herds, in that they do not think of themselves as individuals, but as part of their race; and if the whole race is not threatened, they die with equanimity.

Certainly, *he* showed no lack of equanimity. We put the crossbeam on him (that is the part of the cross the criminal carries to execution; the upright is already fixed in the ground) and we began his last walk. He had lost a great deal of blood in the scourging, and he found the crossbeam heavy. But still he said nothing, until he encountered a group of weeping women who tried to condole with him. Then he said, "Women of Jerusalem, do not weep for me, but weep for yourselves and for your children." And he told them that soon Jerusalem would fall. He said, in fact, that not one stone would be left standing on another.

How did he know that? Is he, in fact, some kind of king? We Romans know very well that if matters do not improve (and they show no signs of improving), there will be another revolt among the Jews, and we will have to take this city and demolish it. It is also our custom, when concluding hostilities with subject peoples who have caused us too much trouble, to lay their cities level with the ground and to sow salt on the ruins so that not even grass will grow there. But how could a Jew know that?

Sometime during our march to the place of execution, a woman came out of the crowd and wiped his face with a cloth; and he said, "Veronica, that was kind and will be remembered." She thrust the cloth with which she had wiped his face into her bosom as if it were something precious. But why should her act be remembered? And how did he know her name was Veronica? I asked him where he had known her before, and he said, "Everywhere."

At last, where the road grew too steep for him, he fell under the crossbeam. As is customary in such cases, I let him have another taste of the whip to make him rise. He looked at me as if he pitied me and not himself, and for some reason I desisted.

In any case, he could not rise. I, therefore, commandeered from among the onlookers a huge black man (I could not, after all, degrade my soldiers with such a shameful task); and the black man snarled at me that he was not even a citizen of Jerusalem, but came from Cyrene, and that he was a free man, not a slave, and that he would not do it. But when I drew my shortsword and held the edge of it to his throat, he stooped and picked up the crossbeam as if it were no more to him than a splinter. And Jesus bar Joseph, breaking his silence, said, "You see, Simon, this cross is very light to you. It is heavy only to me."

The black man said with a curious respect, "Sir, how do you know my name is Simon?"

And Jesus bar Joseph said, "I know everyone who belongs to me."

"Sir, I do not belong to anyone."

"You will, Simon. You will."

By the gods, as strange a conversation as was ever heard. Am I not right in saying that all the Jews are mad?

With the weight taken off his shoulders, Jesus bar Joseph was able to walk, and we climbed up onto the Place of a Skull to find the central upright free but the two others, one on either side, already occupied by criminals who, judging from their thrashing and cursing, must have been on their crosses only a short time. After a few hours, no man has strength to do anything but groan.

We proceeded in the usual way, removing the upright from the earth, affixing the crossbeam to it, stripping the prisoner and nailing him to the wood through his hands and feet in such a way that he could rest part of his weight after the cross was raised upon the little step which protruded from the upright under his buttocks.

In the invention of this little step, the Carthaginians exceeded even the cruelty of their ancestors, the ancient Phoenicians. For because the condemned man can rest much of his weight upon it – and in that way continue to breathe – he lives many hours longer than otherwise.

I do not know why I did it; but at the last moment, before we raised the cross, I drew my shortsword and sticking it beneath Jesus bar Joseph, pried the little step away from the upright and threw it to one side. He understood; and even with his blood pouring over the heads of the nails, he smiled!

It is the custom of the Jews (and one which we, for reasons of diplomacy, accede to in this land) to daze criminals before their execution with myrrh mixed in wine, so that their anguish may be less. But when, after his cross was set into the ground, one of my soldiers held this mixture to the lips of Jesus bar Joseph, he would not drink. This I did not understand.

Neither did I understand the things he said during his torment.

I have been in charge of many crucifixions, and therefore have seen all kinds of men die this death. Some curse, some scream, almost all finally plead for mercy. This one did none of these things. He retained his dignity, his serenity, even (I do not expect to be believed) his kindness towards the human race. He said such things as "Father, forgive them, because they do not know what they are doing." I understand that he must have been talking to his god. But I do not understand how any man on a cross could want his executioners forgiven.

He was also like this: When one of the criminals crucified with him tried to add to his suffering by mockery, he answered nothing. And when the other criminal, impressed by his courage and composure – nay, his love – accepted his claim to be a king and humbly asked to be admitted to his kingdom, he replied, "This very day you will be with me in that other world."

There is much more that I could write, but indeed, the whole affair was beyond belief. I will mention only that some women who were devoted to him stayed close to his cross until he died – but only one man, a young man into whose keeping he gave his mother. Where their love is concerned, women are braver than men.

After Jesus bar Joseph was dead (and I had the distinct impression that we had not killed him without his full consent) Joseph Arimathea, a rich man and a man of standing among the Jews went to Pilate and requested the body, saying that he was willing to bury it in a tomb which he had prepared for himself in his own back garden. The word which this Joseph used in asking for the body is the Greek word showing respect for the body, and the word which Pilate used in granting the request was the Greek word which refers to the body as "garbage."[14] But Joseph Arimathea said nothing, because all he wanted from Pilate was the body.

The women who followed Jesus, assisted by the young man, took the body down from the cross, prepared it for burial, and, with the help of Joseph Arimathea's servants, sealed it in the tomb with a huge rock. The body was intact, its legs not broken,[15] because I had myself, on the pretext of making sure that Jesus was dead, thrust a spear into his side to let his spirit depart more quickly.

But the Jews were not yet done. A delegation of their chief men appeared before Pilate and said, "We must set a watch on the tomb, because that deceiver boasted before

---

[14] The two words are roughly englished "soma" and "ptoma".

[15] It was customary to break the legs of the crucified after death, to ensure that none could escape by any deceit.

his death that in three days he would rise again. And if we are not careful, his disciples will steal the body and then claim that he has risen from the dead."

Pilate said, "Set a watch, then. You have guards from the temple. Make the tomb as secure as you can." But afterwards he called for me and said, "I do not trust these Jews. For all I know, they may connive with the disciples of this Jesus bar Joseph and help steal the body – for nationalist reasons. Take a maniple of soldiers and go guard the tomb with them."

I saluted him, I picked my men, I went to the tomb. And there we remained for the best part of three days.

The tomb had been hollowed out of the living rock on which Jerusalem stands, and the huge boulder sealing its mouth had been brought at great labor and expense all the way from the Kidron Valley which bounds the plateau of Jerusalem on the East.[16] The garden itself was very pleasant, full of plants and birds.

On the dawn of the third day, I was asleep, having left sentries on guard, of course. I was awakened by a shaking of the earth, by a great light (it was some kind of light different from sunlight), and by the groaning of the great boulder blocking the mouth of the tomb; it was being forced out of the mouth of the tomb by something inside. And when the great rock rolled forth into the garden, the light grew so dazzling that I lost my senses.[17]

---

[16] This is imaginary. The site of the tomb is not certainly known, much less the details of its construction.

[17] Although this light is, admittedly, not included in the gospel narrative, it is possible that poetic license may here reflect some truth. Theophanies (appearances of God to people) are usually (cf. Mohammed) described by the recipient in terms of light or (cf. Pascal) in terms of "fire."

Never, even in the most mortal encounters or from the most grievous wounds, have I ever fainted. I did not faint. I was struck down by the light as by a club. So were my men, all of them. So were the Jews who were also watching the tomb. When we came to our senses, there was nothing in the tomb but the cerements of the dead.[18]

I reported this to Pilate, who said, "Have you acquired the madness of the Jews by contagion? Or are you, after all these years of service, disloyal to the emperor? Tell me the truth."

I said, "Prefect, I have told you the truth."

Then Pilate began to tremble with fear; and like most people who are afraid, he became first angry and then cruel. "You," he said, "are disgraced, and reduced from centurion to the ranks. You will surrender your weapons and your badges of rank, and will present yourself to the sentries of the day to be imprisoned. A week from this day, unless I hear the truth from you, you will be decapitated as an enemy of Caesar."

Therefore, here I sit writing in prison on my last day. Very soon they will come for me in their iron-shod boots, perhaps men of my own cohort, carrying the great sword with them; and despite their respect for me, they will like true Roman soldiers lead me out to the block and cut off my head.

I could have told Pilate more. I could have told him, for example, that he does not know what he is fighting. So far as I can see, he is fighting a god. No, not *a* god. *The* God.

---

[18]Modern scholars, holding an "eschatological" view of the resurrection, quite commonly consider the empty-tomb narratives a "theological disaster." But then, they also commonly talk about the "Jesus myth."

Jesus bar Joseph has come to me in prison, just as he was before we killed him. Well, not *just* the same as he was. The same and yet different. He does not need to open doors, and he *shines*!

I have seen the marks of the nails in his hands and feet and the wound of my spear in his side. Yet he has forgiven me and told me that I, like the good thief on the next cross, will be with him today in the other world.

I do not yet know anything about that other world, except that he will be in it – and I am glad to go. In this one, there has been nothing for me but hunger and thirst and wounds, and I am weary of it. But perhaps he can do something about this world, too. I think he can. He somehow overcame it.

Here they come for me. I would like to write my last words just to him: "Lord, I am coming as fast as I can!"

Expulsion from Eden*

The beginning of the Third Chapter of the Book of Genesis:

"Now the serpent was more subtil than any beast of the field which the Lord God had made. And he said unto the woman, Yea, hath God said, Ye shall not eat of every tree of the garden? And the woman said unto the serpent, We may eat of the fruit of the trees of the garden; but of the fruit of the tree which is in the midst of the garden, God hath said, Ye shall not eat of it, neither shall ye touch it, lest ye die. And the serpent said unto the woman, Ye shall not surely die: for God doth know that in the day ye eat thereof, then your eyes shall be opened, and ye shall be as gods, knowing good and evil."

---

*After Erich Fromm, German-born psychoanalyst and author of popular books on psychiatry, including **The Art of Loving.**

Expulsion from Eden

I have heard this text preached on more than often. And always the preacher was grieved at the disobedience of man, and said what a dreadful sin it was to eat that fatal apple.

But today I am not interested in the question whether Adam and Eve were *wicked* to eat the apple. I am interested simply in the fact that they *did* eat it – and in the results.

What this story sets forth is the secret of human life. The story says that once we were innocent and happy in the way that animals are. And since Adam and Eve were driven from Paradise, the story must also mean that man has never after been as contented as he was in the days of his innocence.

But an angel stands forever at the gate of that first paradise, swinging a two-handed sword; and he has God's orders not to let us back in. We do not belong in the garden of innocence with the animals any more. We have eaten the fruit of the tree of knowledge. We have become like gods, knowing good and evil. We will have to go on and find another kind of happiness.

Leaving aside the talking serpent and such-like, this story is quite literally true. Man has not always been what he now is. There must have been long ages during which he shared the paradise of the animals, the paradise of not knowing, the paradise of innocence.

Certainly it is a kind of paradise in which those creatures live whose lives are directed by their instincts, who have never eaten of the tree of knowledge. You may see that paradise any day by looking at a beehive. You will hear the song of a thousand workers who do not know that they are working, and see carried out before your eyes miracles of skill and patience. And "miracles" is what I mean. For God Himself is moving every smallest foot and waving every trembling antenna. God Himself does all things directly for the innocent; and we call this working of God "instinct."

But man becomes man at a point where instinct almost disappears. Man became fully man when he ate of the tree of knowledge and began to act for himself. That is why man is a freak on earth. He is the only creature who can fail to be himself. What God does for the lower creatures through instinct, man must do for himself. He must even (hardest of all) decide what to do. This is what it means to lose the paradise of innocence.

Animals have perfect peace, not in the sense that they do not struggle but in the sense that their struggle is determined for them. Among bees, the drone has only to eat what is given him, to make his nuptial flight, to be accepted or rejected by the queen, and to die. He need not decide whether to do these things, nor how they should be done. And no drone has ever died of a broken heart because the queen refused him. He is a drone; and that says all. His life is given to him complete from the beginning.

But a man has to become a man in his own right. And he can fail to be a man. He must decide what to do and how to do it. That is why he is the most anxious of all creatures – and the strongest. For, lacking any set pattern of existence, he must develop the imagination, the reason and the will to fashion a life for himself. We have indeed become like gods. And this is both the tragedy and the glory of our human condition.

Of course, not everybody likes this situation. When Adam and Eve were driven out of the garden of innocence, they were aggrieved. And mankind is still aggrieved. Watch a baby's face the first few times he discovers he is not living in paradise, and you will see just how aggrieved mankind is. There is no rage like a baby's rage when all his wants are not immediately supplied. And there are times in any man's life when he wishes he did not know good or evil or much of anything else. Most people, in fact, refuse to accept the conditions of human life, and even envy the animals.

The oldest question in philosophy is: Would you rather be Socrates or a pig satisfied? At our lowest and laziest, we would far rather be pigs satisfied. Men do not always enjoy being men. Some of them try to sneak back into the old paradise of innocence. But the angel of God still stands at the gate, swinging his two-handed sword. We will have to go on and find another kind of happiness.

Now: Do you know why a great many people are miserable? Simply because they are looking for a kind of happiness that is impossible for man – and *over*looking the joys that are peculiar to human life.

People complain because they are not as contented as Carnation cows, because they have blue days as well as bright days, because they seem to become holier – and then directly get sinful again.

Well, the only people who ever achieve a permanent calm are the advance schizophrenics in mental institutions. No *normal* person can hope to attain perfect and permanent equilibrium, because even our spiritual advances bring fresh problems with them. For man, *every* advance brings fresh problems.

In this life, as soon as you can drink milk out of a glass, you have to learn about knives and forks. As soon as you have mastered arithmetic, they set you problems in algebra.

And it is the same with every stage of growth. The sinner has to get over criticizing other people, and the saint has to get over criticizing himself – and so it goes. To be human is to find yourself forever on a road that never for one mile remains the same.

Man is a tightrope walker every moment of his life, and must be satisfied that he is, after all, still standing on the wire. He must not care if the wire sways a bit. And if he falls off, then he must climb back on the wire and try again. Only the unwillingness to meet these conditions can make anybody a failure as a human being. But as the once-popular song most profoundly says, "You gotta have heart!"

Man is the only experimenter on earth. And since he has to experiment as other creatures do not, he must expect to make mistakes and to feel sorrows that other creatures never do. Man has been given the responsibilities, but not the powers, of a god. And in this impossible situation, he must be content to do his best. That is all he *can* do; and it is all that God demands.

As for the new kind of happiness that man must find:

A man must realize that his deepest and most lasting joys arise directly out of his sorrows. And that is where we must look for joy to appear – out of sorrow.

There is no spiritual growth whatever without pain. And the gates of heaven are forever locked against those who cannot build their joys upon their agonies. This is the meaning of every pain and misery in human life: that it is necessary, not to God but to man himself, to drive him to a higher form of existence.

Expulsion from Eden

The God who drove us from our first paradise has not left us comfortless. For out of that first tree from which man ate the forbidden fruit has bloomed a second tree, the tree of the cross, whose fruit is forbidden no one. Indeed, we must all imitate Christ, at least by suffering.

Yet that cross is called by those who know it best "sweetest wood and sweetest iron," although it is a torture stake. For out of it has come the deepest happiness man knows, the happiness of trust in God. Through trust in God, even the saddest tragedies of life are transfigured and a new innocence is gained, not less but greater than our first innocence, the innocence of a clean and loving spirit.

Only see how the cross goes up and down from hell to heaven, and how its arms reach out to embrace everything! The cross holds everything together and makes life meaningful and glorious. It shows us how our final happiness is built upon our pain. If we understand the cross at all, we do not simply *endure* pain: we realize that it can bring us closer to Christ; and we offer our brave acceptance of it to God as a sign of our faith in Him.

We have eaten of the tree of knowledge, which was the beginning of our true humanity; and we shall have to go on to the tree of faith, which will perfect us. And faith is the assertion that in all things, even in our sorrows, God intends well; that God is light, and in Him is no darkness at all.

The eating of the apple is called by the theologians "The Fall of Man." But the saints, who know much more about God than the theologians, have exclaimed with one voice, "O happy fall, that brought us such a Saviour!" I think they might have added, "O happy fall, that gave us such a life!"

The Testimony of the Lower Servants

NOTE: The suggestion here set forth that animals reincarnate is, of course, not part of the Christian faith, and is introduced for artistic reasons. But who knows?

It was dawn in the rich man's stable; and Hillel, the ox, stood with his nose out at the raised slat, pointing at the morning star. Hillel's eyes were like dark mirrors. The rising of a great sun or the opening of a perfect flower might be reflected in them, and, at the same time, the thoughts of Hillel, rising and flowering in accord.

So, at least, thought little Jacob, the donkey. He stood rubbing flanks with Hillel, his nose rested on the sill, and watched the dawn grow in his friend's eyes.

"Christmas morning!" said Hillel. "And once more we are together."

"Not like that *first* Christmas, though," said Jacob. "Now that *was* a morning! And the night that came before it was even better." Jacob shut his eyes, just sniffing at the hay scent, remembering, as animals remember best, with his nose. "Yes," he said. "That *was* a morning."

"Be quiet and come down into the fodder until a decent hour," grumbled a deep voice. It was Theophilus, the camel, an habitually late riser. "What is there to talk about at such an hour, anyway?"

"Christmas morning!" said Jacob.

"This is it," returned the camel, as if that settled it.

"But not the first one," said Jacob. "Hillel and I were remembering the first Christmas, and the night that came before it."

There was the awkward sound which Theophilus makes getting to his feet, and then he stood next to them, his sinewy neck hung out the window. He said, in the softest voice that a camel can manage, "You are the ones who were there?"

"Yes," said Jacob. "We are the ones who were there."

Jacob spoke to Hillel. "It is kind of the Lord," he said, "to let us see this one more sun come up together. Our master might have had you slaughtered yesterday; such is the custom. But the Lord stayed his hand, and now I can see you go with a lighter heart."

Hillel lifted his broad nose from the sill and fixed a compassionate eye upon the little donkey. "You must not begin to fear death as men do, Jacob. I, too, am grateful that the Christmas sun rises to find us together. But, for the slaughter, what is it to be slain? It is an instant of pain. It is a moment of falling. But always the Lord catches us in His hand."

Jacob's spirits rose instantly.

"I will not forget that," he said. "My sorrow is only for the long time before we meet again. Sometimes we part for many years. But always, in some cluttered market place or on some straight road near the horizon, we meet to see a Christmas dawn. Then we fulfill our commission. We give our testimony. Let us tell our story."

Hillel looked once more at the sky.

"You are right," he said. "It is time."

And immediately his voice sounded through the rich man's stable so that no beast there could sleep. The goats and the sheep and the dogs that kept watch and the horses and the camels, and every creature that bedded under the straw, came quietly before the donkey and the ox. And they saw so bright a spirit burning in the eyes of these two that they asked no questions. They knew they were to hear the testimony of the Lord's lower servants.

"Know first," began Jacob, "that before the first Christmas, the world spun like a great wheel that has no beginning and no end. The birth of our Lord was like the cleaving of that wheel with an ax, so that the parts are laid out with a beginning and an end. The end of life is still far off. And in the times yet to come will be born many and many men, our masters, whose lives are like the wheel which the ax has split; for the lives of men have a beginning and an end.

"But we animals are like that first wheel which has no end; for, as we depart out of this world, so we are brought back into the world for the perfecting of our duties within the Great Plan of the Lord. Did not our lives spin round and round like wheels, the lives of men could not go along the straight path to heaven. We are beasts that men may be more than beasts. We are the round sky. They are the path of the sun through the sky. They are born once. We are born forever, until the Last Day, when all beasts shall lie down to rest. This is my testimony."

There was no sound in the rich man's stable as Hillel stalked forward and laid his broad nose over Jacob's back.

"It was so, with my nose over Jacob's back, that I, Hillel, saw the coming of the first Christmas. I belonged, not to a good Jew but to a hypocrite and blasphemer, who named me Hillel in spite after a great rabbi in Israel, and who brought me to the town of Bethlehem to slaughter me for the tax. It was in a stable of that town that I met Jacob, the donkey.

"There was a partition raised between our stalls and that part of the stable which was kept lighted for the comfort of the sheep. And when I heard a moaning in the dark of the stalls, coming, as I thought, from the donkey that was there, I rebuked him, saying, 'Be quiet, donkey, lest thou give fright to the sheep and the shepherds come to beat thee.'

"But the donkey rebuked me again, saying, 'Be quiet also, ox, lest the shepherds beat thee in thy turn. It is the woman yonder among the sheep who makes moan, and not I.'

"Then Jacob, for it was he, led me to the partition. And we thrust forth our noses over the top. And there, among the sheep that huddled to give her warmth, a woman labored to bring forth a child. And the very shepherds of Jezreel turned away to shield her from embarassment. But the husband of the woman had removed himself to the very door,where he sat looking at the woman with black looks.

"It was toward midnight that the woman was delivered of her child. And at that hour there broke forth a glad noise through the roof of the stable, so that Jacob and I said to each other, 'Surely the guests are very merry in the inn to forget the tax on the morrow.' But the shepherds trembled greatly and fell on their faces. The husband of the woman was also changed in his bearing towards her, treating her, as became him, with respect. A fortnight later, I have learned, came certain splendid men of magic from the East, who had been forewarned of this birth by the stars; and these treated the child as over them all, for he was very perfect. It is said among men that the night itself had other omens, but I know nothing besides. The morning following, I was slaughtered for the tax money. When next I saw Jacob, the Lord himself was with him. And of this I must tell you.

"I was at that time in my prime strength and belonged to a rich man, one Joseph Arimathea, who lived in the great city of the Jews and worked me on his lands outside the walls. Now, one day in the heat of the sun, I lay beneath a shade tree, for the men were at meat. And I beheld a ragged line of men, few in number but raising an army's dust, coming up the road into Jerusalem. And these men were as if possessed, so that they danced and sang like young cattle. And in their midst came a young man riding upon a donkey which was a colt.

"This was a time of great uncertainty, there being many thousands of the poor who rose in desperation to plunder and fill their stomachs. Therefore I made haste away from the road in fear of being taken from my master. But I had not gone far from the shade tree before the colt called me by name; and in him I recognized the donkey, Jacob, who was with me in the stable in Bethlehem. And at the same instant, with the quickness that a plow cuts two clods, I saw also in the one who rode upon the donkey the child born in that same place. His eye fell on me, and I loved him; and at once he passed by towards the great city, and I saw him no more.

"But on a certain night not long after, Joseph Arimathea came into the stable, weeping. He harnessed me with his own hands, and led me softly into his garden, to the mouth of a great cave that was there to receive the dead of his family. Among the flowers near the cave there lay a body wrapped for burial. And into the mouth of the cave was rolled a stone of such size that no man's strength could take it away, nor the strength of many men. But the weeping of Joseph Arimathea touched me so that my shoulders were like the shoulders of an elephant against the leather harness. And for his sake I pulled away the stone with one great pull, so that my heart broke, and I died."

There was silence in the rich man's stable. Then the sheep said, "The one lying among the flowers was our Lord, was it not? Men killed him just as they kill me."

"Yes," said Hillel. "He is called God's Lamb."

"Ah," said the dog. "Men never know their best friends. It is only because they are a little like him that I love them so. Why do they not all become like him?"

"They are trying," said Hillel. "Ever since he came forth from Joseph Arimathea's tomb, they have been trying. We must be patient. After all, *he* is patient."

There was a step upon the stable floor. The heavy doors into the stalls were flung open, and in the early light a man was seen approaching Hillel.

"Come, patient one," said the man. "Come, symbol of sacrifice, holy beast. You must die to give others life."

He took the ox gently by the halter and led him forth into the yard.

On Meditation*

Every congregation would like, if possible, to have a saint for a minister. And that is understandable. A saint has great charity and deep insight. He can even work miracles.

But there are also some advantages to a minister who is not naturally very religious. He is more like the majority of his people and understands how hard religion is for them.

Obviously, I point to the advantages of the unsaintly minister in my own defense. I am not naturally religious. Religion is very hard for me. In particular, praying has always been hard for me. I like to think about my problems or to work at my problems. I am not naturally inclined to pray about them.

---

*After The Reverend Morton Kelsey, a member of the Department of Religion at Notre Dame.

And so perhaps you will listen when I tell you that lately, because I have been busier then ever, I have spent more time than ever before praying. I even hope you will believe me when I say that fifteen minutes spent praying in the morning can save a man hours during the rest of the day. It cleans a man up. It straightens him out. It pushes him ahead.

Most important of all, prayer is the way to come to love God. You come to love God just as you come to love anyone else – by being with Him. And in prayer you are with Him.

You will find that people who argue about God are confused about Him, but people who pray are not. The people who only talk about God will tell you that religion is a very complicated affair. But the people who pray just smile and remark that God is a very wonderful Person. To the people who pray, religion is no more complicated than any other kind of love.

I have come to the simple conclusion that God is meant to be loved, not to be understood. That is not surprising. Even human beings cannot be understood. I am frank to say, I do not understand anybody; but I love many people. And I intend to act in the same way towards God.

Probably God alone really understands anybody. Certainly, God alone understands God!

The object of religion, therefore, cannot be to understand God. The object of religion must be to *know* God. The loving will take care of itself; for of no other person is it so true to say, "To know him is to love him." And the best method of coming to know God is a form of prayer called MEDITATION.

Now, I know what you are thinking when you read that word, "meditation." You are thinking: "holy men, saints, black cassocks, hard stone floors, guttering candles in medieval monasteries" – all the trappings of the professionally religious. You are thinking that nothing so monkish and nunnish could possibly be any concern of yours.

But as a matter of fact, meditation is the kindergarten of religion; and everybody who gets anywhere in religion goes through it.[1]

Prayer is the raising of the mind to God. And meditation is the simplest and easiest way of raising the mind to God. Of course, the saints have carried it to great heights. But fundamentally it is nothing but withdrawing the mind from trifles and fastening it upon eternal things.

And this, at first, is not so easy to do, even for a short time. The story of St. Francis and the horse shows that meditation takes practice.

Somebody, it seems, had given St. Francis a horse. It was a magnificent animal, and gorgeously decked out. St. Francis, who loved poverty, was embarassed by this expensive horse, and thought only of how to get rid of it.

Soon a chance presented itself. The saint was riding along on his horse, lost in his morning meditation – and almost ran over a man walking in the road. "Why don't you watch where you're going?" snarled the man (pedestrians haven't changed).

St. Francis explained that he was making his morning meditation and was therefore withdrawn from the world.

---

[1] So, in substance, Morton Kelsey in remarks at a retreat in Arizona attended by the author.

"Any fool can do that," said the man.

St. Francis was charmed. "Do you think so?" he said. "Well, if you can sit down and meditate on God for only three minutes, I will give you this horse."

The man thought that was fine. He sat down by the side of the road and began to meditate. One minute went by; a minute and a half; a minute and three quarters. Then the man looked up and said, "Does that include the saddle?"

I often think of that story when my mind wanders in church. For, after all, Sunday morning is our time of times to practice meditation. In fact, the service of Morning Prayer is planned just for that purpose: to assist us in meditating upon God. But I do not expect to make a perfect score even on Sunday morning. And I do not expect it of others.

One of the most saintly ministers of our church once called his acolyte in the middle of the Communion Service and sent him scurrying over to the rectory. In the midst of the most solemn service of the church, this holy man had remembered that he had left a roast too long in the oven.

You must not expect to become perfectly spiritual even at the best of times. And if you do not expect it, you will not become discouraged. People who never get anywhere in religion make the same mistake as people who never get anywhere in music: they look at somebody who is accomplished and say, "Oh, well, he was born that way."

But, believe me, nobody is born a master of the religious life. And the saints have the same difficulties to master that we have. We are all what C. S. Lewis[2] calls "amphibians," half animal and half spirit. And we do not become any less animal just because we are thinking about God. The body is still there, calling for our attention. The poet John Donne writes that he begins a profound meditation upon God – and very soon is thinking about nothing but the hard little pea which has somehow got lodged under his knee.

Do not be discouraged, either, by the "professional meditators," scholarly bishops, etherial sisters, retreat masters, and the rest. They often make this whole business sound impossibly hard. But then, your mechanic is apt to make the repair of your car sound impossibly hard, too. After all, that's his business!

One time when I was in seminary, the Bishop of London came to give a course on prayer. And when he was through, most of us were ready to quit the ministry before we had ever begun. If what he said was true, then we must doubt that we could ever be ministers. What horrible fastings unto prayer! What dizzy soarings of the soul to God! Hours upon hours on your knees. How could we hope to accomplish all this? Most of us had trouble enough praying for ten minutes at a time.

But then the Bishop of London was overheard talking to the Dean of the school. And the saintly bishop said, "You know, I had to start the Lord's Prayer eighteen times this morning before I could get through it once."

You see? You will always remain human, no matter how far advanced in religion. If you do not remain human, then you are not religious – you are *sick*.

---

[2]English writer and Cambridge don (1898-1963).

Now, if you wish to advance in religion you must go about it in a businesslike way and learn it as you learn anything else, by application and practice. And if you wish to benefit much from going to church, you must certainly practice meditation. You would not get ready for church without paying some attention to your clothes. Well, then, pay some attention to the soul you are carrying there.

People fail to get what they need in church because they come in "cold," after a week spent away from God. And much as your minister cares for you, he cannot re-establish in one hour a relationship which you have broken by neglect all week long. If you totally neglected a friend who loves you very much, would you expect the minister or anyone else to make that a joyful relationship on an instant's notice?

Yet if you never speak to God except on Sunday, that is what you are asking. Even the masters of the religious life prepare for worship. They most of all! One of the saints said, "If I had fifteen minutes to worship God, I would spend ten of them getting ready."

And the best way to get ready for church (in fact, one of the best ways to get ready for all eternity) is to do a meditation. And meditating is like playing the violin: there is a right way and a wrong way.

In the first place, meditate only upon Scripture, because the Bible has a mysterious power to convey God to the soul which no other book possesses.

And meditate most upon those parts of Scripture which are beautiful, because God is beautiful; and from one kind of beauty you will go easily to another.

Above all, meditate upon the actions and words of Christ; for the more steadily you look at him, the more real he becomes to you. And the more real he becomes to you, the more you will become like him.

Once you have chosen a passage, try to get the difficulties out of the way. Meditation does not mean arguing with yourself. It means raising the mind to God. If you are vexed by problems in the text, you get nowhere.

What does Christ mean by "love"? Why does he call his followers "the salt of the earth"? Use a commentary to get answers. If the language of the King James version troubles you, use a modern translation of the Bible.

Then read the passage to understand it. Read it several times. Give it a chance to work deep into your mind. Listen to it.

Some ministers, you know, read the Bible in church as if they had written it. But the finest compliment that can be paid any minister on his reading is that he reads the Bible as if he were listening to it.

And that is always the way to read the Bible, to yourself or to others. Listen when you read, because God speaks to you through the Bible, and He may say something to you which He has never said before. You may be surprised. Sometimes, words that you have heard all your life (but not heard) will suddenly *mean* something to you. A meaning which was never there before leaps out from the page.

Now, if you are quietly listening for the voice of God in His Word, you have already left the confusions and distractions of the world behind and already stand in the Presence of God. You have left everything else behind now in order to meditate upon the Word of God.

At this point, go one step further: leave the Bible behind, too, and meditate upon God Himself. Do not make a great exertion of it. Your mind is already lifted up toward God. Let it go by itself, and it will rise the rest of the way.

When God says in Scripture, "Be still then, and know that I am God," this is what He means.

The Incarnation

"And the Word was made flesh, and dwelt among us, and we beheld his glory, the glory as of the only begotten of the Father, full of grace and truth."

John 1:14

I would, today, preach to you the Incarnation, the making-flesh of God in Christ – to see whether, in fact (as I am told), it means nothing to men any more.

Of course, it means *everything* to some men still. It means everything to *me*. But I wish to see whether it means anything to *you*, whether in the face of this most overwhelming evidence of God's humility, men's hearts cannot still be hushed and awed.

If not, if the day is gone by when we can sing in faith "Unto us a boy is born, King of all creation," then let us, in honesty, close this building and go about the business of this world. For then the Faith is dead, and not all the clever language of the most sophisticated scholar will ever make it live again.

Men do not live by cleverness. They live by hard and real things, like bread and the Word of God. And if the Word of God is nullified, then we must live by bread alone.

The Catholic Faith is, in part, called "Catholic" because it makes a universal appeal: it has Good News for *all* men. All types and temperaments of men find God within this faith. And even different cultures have found themselves most at home in one or another aspect of it.

Thus, in the western world, men have customarily best found Christ by gathering on Calvary, at the foot of the cross. There, where God's goodness suffers for man's wickedness and redeems it, the man of the western world has found the kernel, the heart, the illumination of the Faith. But in the Eastern Church, the center of religion has always been the manger.

Since I have from time to time publicly been called "medieval," I will not hesitate to quote some Latin. It is, like so much of the scorned medieval world, majestic and full of faith:

"O magnum mysterium et admirable sacramentum, ut animalia viderunt Dominum natum, iacentem in praesepio. Noe, noe."

"Behold, a great mystery and a wonderful sacrament; that oxen should see the new-born Lord lying in a manger. Noel, noel!"

And, indeed, Christ is himself the very prototype of every sacrament, a visible sign of God's own grace. As for the oxen who saw him in his manger, St. Clement says,

"Christ found men reduced to the level of the beasts. Therefore is he laid like fodder in a manger."

"Behold, a great mystery . . . ."

It is *the* great mystery of our Faith, this laying of Christ in the manger – one that is to some degree repeated every time a child is born and "becomes subject unto the powers of this world." We are not God, like him. And we cannot live perfectly despite the powers of this world, like him. But we are something made for God, nevertheless. And we can follow him.

Christ "took the form of a servant and became obedient unto death, yea, the death of the cross." And his followers are servants, too, and must be obedient unto death, too – and must accept *their* crosses. But the bigger our crosses, it seems, the higher we are lifted toward God. Perhaps we may even draw some men unto Him.

Christ, then, is made man of the flesh of his mother, Mary. But his Father is God.

To say, as has lately been said, that "the evidence indicates that Joseph was the human father of Jesus" is to say nothing that makes any sense. The only evidence there *is* says that his Father was God.

And to know that his Father was God, we have only to look at his life and death and resurrection. Tell me that Joseph was the father of Jesus, and I will tell you that, then, I cannot believe a word of what is written about Jesus. For I am naturally born, and I know that what Jesus did is beyond the power of one naturally born. Either he was supernaturally born, or else he never existed.

Will you tell me that many heroes of the ancient world were reputed to be born of virgins through the agency of gods? And will you tell me that, therefore, there is no reason to believe that Jesus, any more than these others, was virgin-born or born of divine paternity?

That is like telling me that, because the superstitious alchemists of the Middle Ages pretended to do things in their laboratories which they never did, therefore the atom bomb has never gone off!

The tales of the virgin birth and divine paternity from the ancient world reflect the age-old yearnings and abiding intuitions of the human heart. The men of the ancient world told stories of the virgin birth of their mythical saviors because they knew in their hearts that so a real savior must be born.

Does this prove that a real savior has *not* been born? It would be strange if Christ, when at last he did come, did not fulfill the oldest longings and deepest perceptions of the human heart.

The same is true of sacraments.

Are we to abandon the Church because it is rediscovered (which the earliest fathers of the Church knew perfectly well) that in pagan cults were sacraments that looked like ours? Many religions baptized. Many broke bread and drank wine together, seeking identification with some god.

Does this invalidate the sacraments? Do we say that because the first attempts at flying failed, therefore modern planes do not fly?

Why should not Jesus take the outer forms that men already knew – and finally fill them with power? Why should he not take the empty bread and make it his body, the empty wine and make it his blood?

A pagan sacrament was an empty symbol. But a Christian sacrament *conveys what it signifies.* The water of Baptism, by the promise of Christ, really purifies. The bread and wine of the Eucharist, through his power, become at last "the medicine of immortality."[1]

Life was very lonely, once. Men walked here alone, subject to suffering and death, while the gods, with the sublime indifference of Buddhas, smiled above. That was the exact privilege of a god: not to suffer or to die.

It was lonely down here then. It was terrifying. The pathos and the terror of the pagan world are clear to any who will read, and are illuminated by a famous story:

An early Christian was preaching to a pagan king and his court in winter, in a warmed and lighted hall, when in through an open window flew a bird which, after fluttering about a few moments in the warmth and light, flew out another window.

The pagan king said to the Christian, "So is man's life. We come from darkness a little time into the light and warmth, and then return into the darkness again. If anyone can tell me where a man comes from or where he goes, I will listen."

And the Christian said, "Because God has come into the world and told *me*, I can tell *you*. Listen, then. We come from a far brighter light than the light here – and return to Him again."

Who has not heard of the happy days of paganism before Christ was born, before conscience was born to crush men with feelings of guilt? In those days, we are told, men lived with the happy innocence of animals,

---

[1] St. Polycarp, bishop of Smyrna, who died a martyr at the age of 86.

following their instincts, and the world was all a summer garden full of laughing children.

It is lies, all lies. Men had a conscience long before they had a Christ. They had guilt long before they had forgiveness. The pagan world was a dark world, and the ancient religions were dark religions. It was the star of Bethlehem that first lighted up the world.

I can only stare in bewilderment at people who assure me blandly that Christianity leaves them cold, that it is a dull affair which bores them. If they would read the Gospel through just once and let it have its chance with them, they would be compelled to admit, not that it is true, perhaps, but that it is certainly the most exciting story the world has ever heard.[2]

For this is the story of a God who loves us from no great distance, One who loved us enough to become One of us, and has lived through everything that we live through – and won!

This is a God who did not fear to get earth on his hands, and blood, too! And now any man in any fight can put his back to Christ's back and know that, though he may be sore buffeted, he cannot finally go down.

Now we know that, if there is any God at all, He is Christ-like! For Jesus is "the brightness of His glory and the express image of His Person."

Now we know that the very essence of God is not really His power or His majesty or His justice or His wrath, but a loving humility beyond human imagining or human strength, the kind of loving humility which, in the

---

[2] I share the sentiments of G. K. Chesterton.

Incarnation, could bring God willingly into this hard world as a little child.

"Behold, a great mystery and a wonderful sacrament . . . . ."

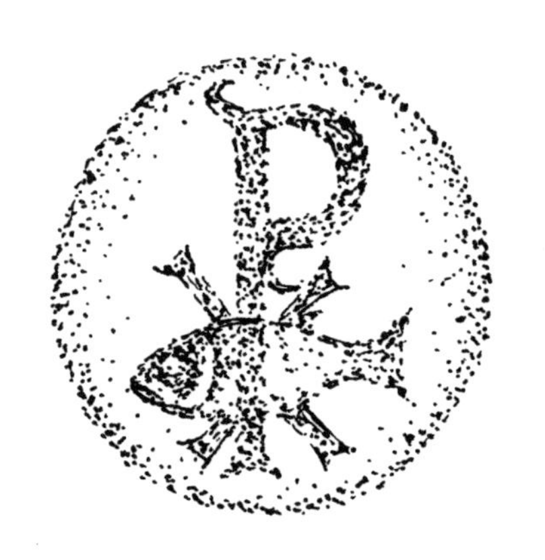

A Dory, a Donkey and a Drink

Lord Christ was born on Christmas Eve, and gave men everything he had – and asked for very little. In all his life, so far as I can find, he asked for just three things: a *dory*, a *donkey* and a *drink*.

A dory:

A dory is a simple little fishing boat.

Matthew 13: "On that day went Jesus out of the house and sat by the seaside. And there were gathered unto him great multitudes, so that he entered into a fishing boat; and all the multitude stood on the beach. And he spake to them . . ."

A dory is nothing very much (it is named after an insignificant little fish), but he would have taken any boat they offered him. He needed a place to stand. A man who is sent by God to tell the Good News has to have a place to stand. One man gets a high place, another a low place.

But, to a man sent by God, the Message is the only thing that matters.

Look at the infant Christ in the stable at Bethlehem and read what the Message is: the hands that made the sun and the stars are too small to reach the huge heads of the cattle![1] At Bethlehem two most remote ideas come together in a fact: the idea of a baby and the idea of the unknowable strength that sustains the stars. So then, the Message is: THE GREATEST POWER HAS THE GREATEST LOVE.

If the men who lent Christ that dory had wanted it back, Christ would simply have asked for another. One dory is as good as another. Dories are no fun to stand in, anyway; they are too narrow at the bottom. Also, the owners of dories have a habit of leaving them half full of filth: entrails and heads of fishes, dead bait, and old mud that should have been washed off long ago.

Dories are seldom clean. They are meant for fishing, not for looks; and fishing, whether for fishes or for souls, is often a dirty business. And so, Christ might have stepped daintily around and held his nose against the stench of that dory as some men hold their noses at the faults of his Church. But I suppose Christ never even noticed the dirt at his feet. He was too full of the love of God to dwell on the faults of men. That was Christ's way. Therefore that is THE way!

A donkey:

A donkey is a little beast of burden with long ears and a harsh bray.

---

[1] G. K. Chesterton, **The Everlasting Man.**

Matthew 21: "And when they drew nigh unto Jerusalem and came unto Bethphage, unto the Mount of Olives, then Jesus sent two disciples, saying unto them, Go into the village that is over against you and straightway ye shall find a donkey tied: loose him and bring him unto me. And if anyone say ought unto you, ye shall say, The Lord hath need of him . . ."

A donkey is a gentle, patient beast, often mistreated. On a donkey's shoulders, formed by contrasting light-colored hairs, you can see the Sign of the Cross.

Only those who come in peace and humility come on donkeys. Those who come in worldly pride come on war-horses – war-horses of flesh or war-horses of steel. And Christ chose a donkey to carry him in his triumph on Palm Sunday because he knew what kind of triumph it was – the triumph of God made small over man made large.

And, O God, before he came in this humble triumph, what infinite mad triumphs had not passed through the cities of men! What pleasure barges floated on lakes of blood and tears! What grinning apes of cruel tyrants carried on the shoulders of sad, downtrodden men! What, in the way of worldly pride, had the world not seen! And what had it all come to? To this: that God had at last to make Himself so small in Christ that pride-swollen man might be ashamed. For Christ on the donkey still means this: THE GREATEST POWER HAS THE GREATEST LOVE.

As for the donkey: it is not irreverent to say, Christ must have felt a kinship of spirit with the little beast that carried him. For the donkey was only doing what God had sent him into the world to do. And it was no concern of his that today he walked on palm branches and bore the Lord Christ on his back; tomorrow, perhaps, would be cursed and beaten. And indeed, it could not matter. For who will mind a few curses or a few blows, having once carried Christ a few paces further into this world?

I like to think that Christ blessed his donkey: legend says that is how the donkey received the cross upon his shoulders. I like to think that Christ talked to his donkey as St. Francis would have done, and said to him, "Little brother, the mood of men changes, but the will of God does not. We will seek to do the will of God and not fear what men can do to us. For men are cruel only because they are afraid. And we will take away their fear by showing them the love of God." That was Christ's way. Therefore that is THE way!

A drink:

A drink of vinegar.

John 19: "After this, Jesus, knowing that all things were now finished, saith, I thirst. There was set there a vessel full of vinegar: so they put a sponge full of vinegar upon a stick of hyssop and brought it to his mouth. When Jesus therefore had received the vinegar, he said, It is finished: and he bowed his head and gave up his spirit."

The Cross, not Palm Sunday, was his triumph, the triumph of love over cruelty. Not when men acclaim us but when they revile us can we show them our love. For, "If you love them that love you, what do ye more than others?" And Christ has been able to show us, even on the cross, that his message is true: THE GREATEST POWER HAS THE GREATEST LOVE.

As for the vinegar: this was not the vinegar we know. Vinegar, in the ancient world, meant any cheap wine of the sour variety. The Roman Army drank nothing but "vinegar" in the field. And at executions it was Jewish custom to mingle myrrh with the vinegar, to stupefy the victim and so give him a more merciful death.

Myrrh was offered Christ at his birth – and at his death. But Jesus refused the vinegar with myrrh until the very end when, as St. John says, "he knew all things were now finished." And when he asked for it he was already very nearly dead, and was not asking for it to escape his pain.

Why did he ask for it, then? *Just to see if anybody cared.* And someone did. Someone always does. And someone who cares – anybody in the world who cares – can make up for all the rest who don't. Which is to say: only in his love can man approach the infinities of God.

And I have not the slightest doubt that Jesus died upon his cross, not only with his faith in God unbroken, but with his faith in men unbroken, too. For some loved him – and some still love him – and some will always love him. And human love, it is so great a thing, it can outweigh even human cruelty. Human love, it is so great a thing that, even on his cross, Christ did all he could to forget the hatred and to bring out the love. That was Christ's way. Therefore that is THE way!

Next time you are tempted to say to God, "O God, give up this awful experiment of trying to make men like Christ! You ask too much, O God!" – next time you are tempted to say that, remember what God in Christ really did ask – and does ask: a place for His messenger to stand, some humility, and a little love to answer His great love for us. That is all. Just a dory, a donkey and a drink.

Ordination Sermon

I do not think this is a time for preaching, but for plain instruction. And so I will not vex the candidate by interpreting all the Scriptures generally used on these occasions, and I will not increase his nervousness by asking him to stand.

Neither will I make a separate address to the laity, as if they were unable to take an interest in the very thing which brings them here. The clergy are not some exalted species, apart from the laity. We separate ourselves from the laity, when we do, to our own cost and humiliation.

The Sacred Ministry is a mystery in just the same way that any Christian calling is a mystery. The mystery is why God should love us so! That is a mystery, indeed! And so, I will go on at once to something more within our grasp, namely your usefulness to God.

Your usefulness to God depends upon His help. You cannot really do anything for God unless you give yourself to Him for His use. And it is beyond a man's natural strength to give himself to God. That is why we speak, hopefully, of "the grace of Holy Orders."

Apparently, it is the laity who believe most firmly in the grace of Holy Orders, they expect so much of us! But we had better believe in it, too. For upon our unshakable confidence in the help of God depends our whole ministry.

I do not know what motives may have brought you to this point, and I do not think your motives greatly matter. If you can explain why you want to be a minister, you are probably deluded; and if you cannot, you are no worse off. Your reasons and your lack of reasons must equally be put away now, together with other childish things. From now on, your reason for everything must be God.

It is enough that you have been brought to this point – by God, we trust. And now you stand as Peter once stood: in a rocking boat, screwing up your courage to walk to Christ across the water. For water it is on which you will walk. And you can walk this water only by faith.

The whole condition of the Christian world is fluid; there are mighty few rocks to stand on anywhere. And our boat, the Church, does rock. O, how she rocks! And in our boat are apostles of this and apostles of that; but, as always, too few Apostles of Christ.

C. S. Lewis says truly, *We* are the "early Christians." What, after all, are two thousand years in the history of the human race? We are still trying to find out who Christ is and what he wants done. And let no man tell you that this is already known. Not the thousandth part of it is known. Let no one tell you, "This or this is the right way because it was so for the first three centuries." God has not stopped speaking.

You are not beginning a slumber in an institution, but an adventure in personal religion. Here you are, about to be ordained a minister. And it is by no means settled what a minister is or what he should do. You must learn that from God.

Nevertheless, in this quest you are going on, there are two things I would advise you to avoid. And the first is this: I would not be ambitious.

If you are an ambitious minister, you are simply telling everybody that you do not believe what you say. And what is worse, you will be prevented by your ambition from saying or doing anything of real worth.

An ambitious man is always in captivity to his ambition, and does not dare to endanger his future hopes by his present actions. An ambitious man could be bought at any time by anybody – if he had not already been bought at a bargain counter by the Devil.

The Devil is an accommodating fellow, and accepts the price we establish.

Do you want a large, rich parish? That, perhaps, can be arranged. But if you desire to be *Rector* of a parish, that, believe me, ambition and the Devil combined can never arrange. For the Rector of a parish must be the one man in it who is equally above its poverty or its wealth, its praises and its threats, its worldly success or its apparent failure. And if at any time you get a parish because you sought it, do you not see that you will be, not the Rector of it but the *creature* of it? For we are the creatures of whatever we desire. That is why it is wise to desire God first.

But, second: I would not seek "saintliness" any more than I would follow ambition, because the desire for saintliness is a kind of ambition and leads to the same perils. It is always safe to try to be like Jesus. But it is never safe to try to be "saintly," because, before you know it, you will be trying to convince other people that you are!

The "saintly Christian character" is largely a prototype invented by men. Most of the men we call saintly are merely men of mild disposition with good digestions. And the trouble with *real* sanctity is that you never know when you have it!

Your real sanctification lies in becoming what God wants *you* to be. And what God wants you to be may not look to you or to anybody else like saintliness at all! But there is nothing so stifling to real goodness as the popular notion of what is good.

Have some confidence in yourself – because you have confidence in God. There are as many kinds of holiness as there are men. And if you are going to imitate the goodness of some other man, there is very little reason for your being here at all!

God wants *your* sort of goodness, *your* possibilities brought to perfection. And each one of us finds his own best self in the imitation of the only one who is truly good, Jesus Christ.

The ministry is, above all, personal. It is the mediation of a Person through a person to persons.[1] And the impact of the Gospel as it comes through you depends somewhat

[1] Phillips Brooks, an Episcopal bishop and author who lived from 1835-1893.

on how much of you there is. Not even God can wash out men's souls with an eyedropper!

So much for the things I would caution you not to do. There are also things that I *would* do. And first, I would master the Gospel. For (peace to all those who think otherwise) the Church exists first and foremost to declare the Gospel.

The Gospel is the treasure committed to us. It is God's own declaration of His love to men through Christ. And you are sent to show this Christ to other men.

I beg you will not "bind on men's backs burdens grievous to bear," but that you will show Christ as he is, a Lord of mercy and not of condemnation. The people in this world, I assure you, are staggering under a sufficient load of guilt and anxiety. You need not add to it by pretending that God is a harsh Judge. There is no priestly sin more heinous than to seek power over men through their fear when we have been sent to give men power over themselves through the love of God.

And, through taking the Gospel to heart, I would seek the greatness of humility. Humble – great: these two words belong together. Without humility, there is no greatness worthy of the name, and certainly none permitted to the clergy.

Humility is moral realism. The difference between any two men in the sight of God never is that one is good and the other bad. The difference always is that one is weak in this way and the other in that. "There is none righteous, no, not one." But all (each for his own reasons) stand equally in need of forgiveness; all equally need the Gospel.

It is only when we understand this that we are freed from our conceited hopes and faithless despairs alike.

Humility alone gives us the generosity of spirit which places us above such "elephant dances" as church parties and above those sad fashions of the world which belong to our particular social and economic background.

In brief, humility creates the courage for Christian action. And the most vexed question in the Church today is this: What *is* Christian action?

Some of our brother clergy appear to think that Christian action means civil disobedience and preaching against Rhodesia. And, no doubt, such actions (if undertaken in one's private capacity) may sometimes be pleasing to God. But if I may be so bold, Christian action must basically mean acting like Christ. And Christ, pretty much ignoring the politics and economics of his day, spent his ministry fishing for the souls of men.

In the souls of men, there is something final and indestructible which answers to God. There is, in fact, some divinity in the souls of men. It can be corrupted, but it is there. It can likewise be converted and transformed. But it will not be either converted or transformed by any change in outer circumstances. It will be converted and transformed only through asking and receiving the power of God. Our task is to make this asking and receiving possible – through the Gospel.

The clergy of our time, by abandoning the preaching of the Gospel in favor of practical problems, have left men without guidance in their practical problems. The voice of the Church today is too often only the weak echo of the voice of the masses. The question is not whether our practical problems are morally important. The question is whether speaking to such practical problems is the proper public office of the minister of Christ.

What we need is the sound of a Voice which is not our voice, but a Voice coming from Someone not ourselves. It is the task of the minister to hear this Voice and to tell his people what it says. If the minister cannot hear it, or if he fails to tell his people what it says, he has no reason to exist. Without this Voice from God, we are no more capable of redeeming the world than we were capable of creating it in the first place.

This, Friend, is a tough life. But if we hear and obey God, it is still the highest calling.

We who come to welcome you into the ranks of Christ's clergy will pray for you. And do you pray for us!

The Monk of the Silver Bell*

There was once, way up at the top of the Himalayas (the greatest mountains of all), a man called Puron-Das who was a monk and a Buddhist and a sage and a lover of God. He was all of these things, and very old besides. But he was most of all a lover of God, which means that other things mattered hardly at all to him. He had only one possession, a silver bell, and this because it kept off the evil spirits, leaving him alone with God.

For he had always sought God. He had sought Him in the statue of Buddha and in the smell of incense and in the beauty of silence. He had spent his life in teaching other men to look for God way up at the top of the Himalayas. And it troubled his soul as he grew older

*Reprinted with permission from the **Arizona Republic,** where this story originally appeared in one of a series of columns entitled "Orthodox" by the author.

that he knew God no better than he did. He called God the "one" and the "none" and the "enlightenment" and the "negation" – that is the way they talk in the East. But these words feel better on the tongue than in the heart. Puron-Das had a great heart, but it was empty.

Sometimes he went out of the monastery and sat at the top of the Himalayas (the greatest mountains of all). He sat so still that the wild deer came to him fearlessly, and the little bear came to him without mischief. And together they sat looking for God. At such times, Puron-Das felt that God was very close. Out of the cold silence of the mountains sprang a warm feeling he knew was God; but it was only a feeling. Once he looked, and saw that the eyes of the wild deer were filled with awful joy, the same joy that was in his own heart. And in that moment he realized that he knew God only as every creature knows God, not as a man should know Him. Puron-Das realized; and he cried out into the void, "What IS God?"

Then the wild deer snorted at the sacrilege of silence, dashing for the forest, and the little bear ran in terror; and only an echo of "God" came back to find Puron-Das alone.

Still he grew older day by day, knowing as little as the day before. He walked bent heavily upon a staff. Soon, he knew, his soul would go out of him, up from the top of the Himalayas; and whether the Maker of souls would receive him, he could not tell. Little by little, the towering peaks of the Himalayas faded dim before his eyes. And with the mountain tops faded his sense of God. In these eternal hills he had felt the Eternal One. Now God fled beyond his sight. When the light is gone, thought Puron-Das, I shall walk alone in the darkness. And for all that he was a monk and a Buddhist, he despaired in his old age.

But one day his heart filled with hope. A traveler stopping at the monastery told him of a new faith which was believed in the plains of India. Perhaps, thought Puron-Das, somebody has found God. I will go down and find Him, too.

Then Puron-Das took his long staff and went down through a pass in the Himalayas, ringing his silver bell to keep off the evil spirits, down into the plains of India. There he found those who believed the new faith. They called themselves the Jains. And indeed they seemed to have found God; for they recounted to Puron-Das all those things that were right and all those things that were not right.

But you must not forget that Puron-Das was a Buddhist and a sage. Therefore he questioned the Jains carefully.

"Why," he asked them, "do you walk with brooms in front of you, sweeping the place where you put your feet?"

"Lest we trample upon insects," said the Jains. "All life is sacred."

"But look yonder at the river," said Puron-Das, "There I see Jains catching fish in nets. Are not the lives of fishes sacred?"

"As for the fish," explained the Jains, "the nets catch them; and when they are drawn upon the bank, they very unfortunately die. But we do not kill them."

Then the old Buddhist's heart fell in him and he saw that he had worn down his staff in vain. "I will go back to my monastery," he said, "and worship my Buddha statue. It is better for me to die in innocence than to learn such deceit." And he went back up to the top of the Himalayas.

But one day another traveler came to the monastery and told Puron-Das of still another faith which was believed in the plains of India. "This faith," declared the traveler, "worships no idols, but the Living God Himself. And those who believe this faith die without fear, they are so sure of God. Indeed, they seek death so boldly that half the world rings with the noise of the wars made for their God."

When Puron-Das heard these words, a measure of hope returned to him. Surely, he thought, no man would fight wars for a God he did not know. I will go down and find what is in God which makes men die without fear. Thereupon, he took up his long staff once more and went down through a pass in the Himalayas, ringing his silver bell to keep off the evil spirits, down into the plains of India.

He was not long in finding the new believers; for, as the traveler had said, half the world was filled with the noise of their wars. They called themselves Islam, the followers of Mohammed the camel driver. They made war on all who did not accept their God, and they swore by the coffin of Mohammed, suspended between heaven and earth.

But Puron-Das was not one to be overborne by the screaming of war horses or the clashing or armor. He had sat with the wild deer and the little bear at the top of the Himalayas; and he sought God quietly.

He asked what God had promised which made men glad for death, and he found a dreadful thing. The heaven promised by the camel driver was a heaven of the five senses. It was an everlasting carousal. There the soldiers of Islam thought to be perfumed with rare flowers and to linger eternally in the arms of unearthly-fair women. And when Puron-Das heard and understood these things, he thought he never would regain the top of the Himalayas, disappointment burrowed so deep in his heart.

"Am I to believe that God offers only this?" he cried. "Has God no riches but the riches of the body? I am already old in this body. Already my eyes ache with seeing, and my ears ache with hearing. I will go back to my monastery and die looking for God. The little bear knows more of God than your camel driver!" And because he was extremely old, they let him go home.

There he had hoped to die in peace; but one day when the light was nearly gone, yet another traveler stopped at the monastery.

Now Puron-Das was in the fullness of his age, having a heart full of unsatisfied longing. When he heard that a traveler had stopped at the monastery, his fear rose that he might be disappointed again. "Do not let him near me!" he cried, "lest he break my heart with fresh sorrow. Let me go in peace."

But the brothers of the monastery soothed his fears, saying, "Here is nothing to break thy heart, Wise One, but only a present for thee from the traveler." And they gave him a book which the traveler had left.

It was some time before Puron-Das considered the book; for now that his hope of finding God was gone, his interest in all things was small. But one day he picked up the book and read. At first he read quickly and not attentively. The story was of a man sent to earth by God; and the man called himself the Son of God.

This man was as penniless as Puron-Das himself. He had not even a silver bell to keep off the evil spirits. He taught men to love God, as Puron-Das taught. This, thought Puron-Das, is no new story. Life is hard for those who seek God. And he moved to put the book away.

But then a strange thing happened. He could not stop reading – because he loved the man in the book. He seemed to recognize the man in the book as one whom he had loved for many years. He sat reading. He followed the man in the book into the desert, into the cities of men, even into men's hearts. And sometimes the words brought a chill to the back of his neck, such a feeling as he had known years earlier when the mystery of God had most overwhelmed him. And at last, when darkness lay over the face of the whole land, he followed the man in the book to his death. They took the man and nailed him up between two thieves; and he died. He died.

Over and over Puron-Das re-read the death of the man, over and over again until the mist grew thick before him and his tears fell steadily upon the page. Dead? Was this all? Was this the end of him who called himself the Son of God? No, thought Puron-Das. This man lied.

And at this he saw that hope had been reborn in him to die more cruelly than every before. "Fool!" he cried. "Fool, to be caught in the error of hope! What reason have I to hope?"

And now Puron-Das fell so down in spirit that death prepared his face for the grave. But he could not forget the man in the book for all his misery in him. "Bring me the book!" he would cry from his bed. "Bring me the book of the fisher of men, that he may fix his hook in my tired heart."

Now one day the brothers of the monastery, amazed at their master's love for the book and pitying the pain he suffered in reading it, talked together by his bed. "How is it," asked one, "that our master has never finished this book? He reads so far, and then he weeps; but he never finishes."

What the others would have answered we shall never know, for Puron-Das had heard. He rose in his bed, and such a look of hope and dread came into his face as never before was seen at the top of the Himalayas – or since. "It is true," he whispered. "I have never finished. Perhaps God is not finished, either."

By his own will he left his bed and went out to finish the book at the top of the Himalayas . . . . "The first day of the week cometh Mary Magdalene early, when it was yet dark, unto the sepulchre, and seeth the stone taken away from the sepulchre . . . . "

The Seven Last Words

We do not meditate upon the last words of Christ as on the last words of famous men.

The last words of men are often beautiful, sometimes clever, even prophetic. Just before he was killed, Stonewall Jackson said to those who rode with him, "Let us cross over the river and rest in the shade." Heine, the skeptic, said on his deathbed: "God will forgive me: that's His profession."

But such words, after all, come to nothing. They are, at best, the last spirited gesture of the little human soul in its house of flesh – and, at worst, cheap defiance of our common fate.

How different are the words of Christ from the cross! The mystery which is in him – the "mystery of godliness" – is in his final words. These words, like him, are immortal and breathe out eternity.

The seven last words of Christ are not important merely because someone speaks them in the grip of death. They are not merely the effort of another great man to sum up in his last few breaths the price he puts upon existence. Had the words of Christ from the cross been like the dying words of men, we would long since have stopped meditating on them. The words would long since have been exhausted, bled to death.

The seven words from the cross endure and continue unexhausted because they are like the rest of Scripture: they are revelation, a sign from God. They are revelation, which means: God showing us something which He alone knows. They have bottomless depths of meaning because, as even a casual glance at them will show, they are by design. The seven last words are no more the result of chance than was the birth of Jesus.

The first three words from the cross are addressed to the three spiritual classes of men (have you ever noticed that?): to the sinner, to the penitent, and to the saint.

To the sinner: "Father, forgive them, for they know not what they do."

To the penitent: "Today shalt thou be with me in Paradise."

To the saint: "Woman, behold thy son."

With a view toward the three spiritual classes of men addressed, and in the order presented, one needs little imagination to see the progression that is suggested: the whole long road from sinner to penitent to saint, which is the way of the cross and of salvation.

Everyone is first of all a sinner. Everyone may become, any day, a penitent. Everyone must finally be (as I believe) a saint, either in this life or in the next. I do not believe that any man can resist God forever.

But as things are now . . .

The First Word

I suspect, however sadly, that most of us will hear Christ's word to the sinner (that first word of all) with more understanding than we hear the rest. For we understand the Gospel only as we are ready in heart to receive it. And God knows, few of us are either penitent or saintly at heart.

Nevertheless, it would be something to think (if we can bring ourselves to think it): "I am a sinner; and Jesus Christ has a word for me, too – even on the cross." To think so would be half way to penitence and a good half way to saintliness. For, you see, the sinners who stood around that cross did not really hear this word on their behalf. They were like us: they did not consider themselves sinners. May we do better and hear the word: "Father, forgive them, for they know not what they do."

Forgive them for what? For crucifying Christ.

Do I speak of the Jews? Well, I speak of them first. We know what dreadful thing they did, they and the cold Romans. And we know what dreadful thing they said, the Jews to the Romans: "His blood be on our heads and on our children."

But have not the Jews suffered enough? Have they not come forth wonderfully strong and purified from all these centuries of beating on the anvil of God? I sometimes think the blood of Christ will save more of them by beating on their heads than it will save of us, to whom it is given free.

And do you imagine that all this infinity of blood and blame can fall on the Jews alone, simply because they were there to crucify him instead of us? Oh, we would do it, never fear. This is the proof that we would do it: we do it every day.

How happy a matter, how happily over and done with, if this crucifixion were all "far away and long ago." It would be a business over which we could become comfortably emotional. We could indulge ourselves in "the luxury of cheap melancholy." We could say, "How I love that gentle Savior hanging on the cross. How cruel they were to him." And we might weep a little. But really, so long as you think it was all far away and long ago, it does not greatly matter.

But now, THINK! If Christ is alive (and no one is so alive as he), then he can still be crucified. And that is what happens.

Stedderet Kennedy[1] says, and says truly, that when Christ came to Golgotha they crucified him. And that was hard. But when Christ came to Manchester in modern England, the people simply passed him by. And that was harder still. He holds out the host and the chalice, and the people go by. He says, "Is there any sorrow like my sorrow?" His sorrow is that he holds out himself to the people, and the people he loves go by.

For, look you, he is crucified, and we make it all in vain. Our colored brothers are right, who sing:

"Were you there when they crucified my Lord?
"O, sometimes it makes me tremble, tremble . . . . "

It should. God knows, sometimes it makes me tremble. For I am as guilty as the High Court of the Jews, as guilty

---

[1] A famous British Army Chaplain who served in the First World War and was afterwards (for an Anglican) considered a great evangelical preacher.

as Pontius Pilate, as guilty as the one Roman who drove in the spikes and the other who drove in the spear.

Why do I say that I am guilty of the crucifixion? Why do I say (which is much more and much worse) that you are? I say it because it is the evil in man which crucifies Christ that first time – and then again and again and again.

Look 'round you and see. Look beneath the pleasant surface of society, the society men have built after two thousand years of the cross. Look and see! Our whole society is built over a reeking slaughterhouse.

Or listen: underneath the most polite symphony concert you will hear the screaming of the wild beasts, the human wild beasts, feeding on each other. Oh, this horrible abyss between the gentle manners of society and the obscene cruelties on which it stands!

Under every loving brotherhood a hatred of some other brother. Under every wealth, want. Back of every loaded food counter the spectre of starvation elsewhere. Back of every quiet hour the growling of the guns.

Above all, pretense, pretense, pretense! Our public morals are more pretentious than the Monastic Rule of St. Benedict; but we have the private morals of Bengal tigers. It is one of the wonders of history and one of the evidences of Divine Providence that we have not exterminated the human race.

We crucify him this way: with selfishness, with lovelessness, with hypocrisy. Every one is a nail, a lance, vinegar on a stick.

So often in my parish someone comes to me and says, "Why are you so hard on people? Who are you to judge people so harshly?" Or someone says, "I am sick to death of hearing myself called a sinner. Who are you to say I am a sinner? Are you any better?"

No, friends, I am no better. And surely you know that I do not say these hard things because I have a low opinion of my fellowman. It is just the other way: I think so highly of my fellow man that, very often, I see the Christ in him. And I cannot endure to see us crucify each other – that is what I am talking about. I see in this crucifixion of Christ the crucifixion of us all. It is not only our Lord Christ who is tortured by our inhumanity: it is all of us.

If only you could live my life a few short days, you would be overwhelmed, as I am, by the suffering nearly everyone endures. Most men, truly, live "lives of quiet desperation."[2]

So long as I do not know a man, I see him walking by, and he looks as if he had no burdens. But after I become his minister, I know his burdens; and when I see him walking by I pray for him, and that his brothers may stop crucifying him and begin to love him. For the sad truth is, almost all our suffering is imposed on us by other people.

And I have a vision of what this world of men might be if, in every man, we could see the Christ that is there, and if we could extend to the Christ that is in our neighbor a little of the reverence that we say we have for Christ. I have a vision of what our life might be if, in place of judgment, we gave our understanding and love.

Our sin is in our thoughtless cruelty, and the habit we are in of seeing in everybody what he means to us rather

---

[2]Henry David Thoreau, **Walden.** "The mass of men lead lives of quiet desperation."

than what we might mean to him. And I beseech you by the crucifixion of our Lord to drive in no more nails or spears, but to take the Christ that is in every man you know down from the cross with all reverence and love.

The Second Word

Thus he speaks the first word on behalf of sinners. And that we would expect of him. The sad, the hurt, the lost were always uppermost in his mind.

But the second word which Christ speaks from the cross, he speaks to the penitent, to the penitent thief on the next cross – to him and to all the penitent thieves who shall ever come after him.

This thief has watched the nobility of Christ through the agony of crucifixion, and seen the miracle of Christ's love for those who torture him. And though the other thief, the one crucified on Christ's other hand, rails at Christ and curses, this one is softened to repentance by Christ's love, and says to him, "Lord, remember me when thou comest into thy kingdom." And Christ says, "Today shalt thou be with me in Paradise."

I say the words that Christ speaks from the cross are not by chance, but by design: they were determined and intended by God. How can it be otherwise? For do you not see how suitable it is that the repentant man on the next cross is a thief? Before we repent, we are all thieves.

A thief is one who takes things from their rightful owner. A sinner is one who takes some part of God's world away from God, to use it for himself alone. Therefore, you see, a thief is a sinner, and a sinner is a thief.

What a pity to sin by stealing or to steal by sinning! It is all done in vain. You finish on the cross of death. You finish penniless. For the things that belong to God return back to God like iron filings to a magnet. And everything that exists belongs to God, so that at the end you possess nothing but your own soul. And if your soul is not rich towards God, you will be penniless indeed.

Therefore the Hindus say: "The earth is the living garment of the Lord. Renounce it, and receive it back as the gift of God."

That is to say: God must give you what is truly yours. Whoever by stealth or violence or manipulation grabs any part of the creation for himself, is tearing the very shirt off God's back. He is a thief, indeed! And what he steals is never truly his. God must give us what is truly ours. Only in this way does man possess anything.

Anything or anyone.

I may love a woman so that I can scarcely eat or sleep, so that I am all hollow inside, so that I am like a man dying of thirst in a desert. I may tell her (and it may be true) that never, anywhere will anyone love her as I do. But if God does not put it into her heart to love me back, she will not love me back. For love is a miracle. And miracles come from God.

What shall I do, then? Threaten to cut my throat? Change my toothpaste? Make a lot of money? Try to convince her that she does love me?

Alas, if any of these things should work! Alas for me as well as for her. Because she will never belong to me unless she truly loves me. And she will never truly love me unless God wills it. If she does not come to me simply because she cannot do otherwise, I have stolen her – and will not keep her.

If by stealing you hope to possess what is stolen (and that is why men steal), forget it. You cannot finally have it. All things are eternally in motion; and the motion of all things is towards God. Unless you are with God, all things, moving towards Him, struggle at last out of your hands.

Or if by sinning you hope to possess joy (and that is why men sin), forget it. You cannot finally have it. There is no joy in sin. Otherwise, the devils might have it.[3]

The joy which God gives you, that is your joy, and no other. But God is not niggardly. He is ready to give you nothing less than Paradise.

Paradise: the condition of those who are to enter heaven.

Paradise means at least this: the beginning of eternal life. This is where the penitent thief goes; and he goes there today! Christ says to him, "Today shalt thou be with me in Paradise."

Ah! Would it not be Paradise, indeed, to renounce all hatred and all jealousy and all self-centeredness? Would it not be Paradise to see and value other persons as they are in themselves, and to stop seeing and valuing everything and everybody only as they affect me? Would it not be Paradise to learn what love is: that love is a condition in which the other person's happiness is necessary to my own?

If I could learn these things, then Christ could say to me, "Today shalt thou be with me in Paradise."

How could this happen? Let me explain:

---

[3]St. Thomas Aquinas.

The Kingdom of God is something we shall see after death, yes. But it is there to see after death because it is there always. We see the Kingdom of God after death simply because we do not look for it before death, that is all. The Kingdom is all around us now, as God Himself is. But we see neither the Kingdom nor its King.

The Kingdom of God will come with a power and a glory that all men can see on Judgment Day. On Judgment Day, God will invade the visible world once more and set up His kingdom as the visible government of this world. There will be no one who cannot see it.

But it will appear in that awful Day of Judgment that the Kingdom of God was here always, open to us, and that certain men, at least, have walked into it in life, not waiting until they died to enter into the joy of Paradise. It will appear that Jesus told us true: "The Kingdom of God is among you . . . . The Kingdom of God is (potentially) within you . . . . It is here! . . . . Now! . . . . Enter into it!"

And many people have done this. Some, like St. Dominic, are famous – St. Dominic, who was so much a citizen of the Kingdom of God that he was ready to renounce even Paradise itself for love of other men, and prayed God that he might be a stone, blocking the mouth of hell.

Most who have done this are not famous. But they are always recognizable.

You may know them by their readiness to love and their refusal to hate; by their child-like (not childish) openness; by the way they laugh, not *at* but *with* the other foolish people in this world.

By a basic serenity which proves that they have been with God enough to trust Him; by their contempt for manipulation; by their calm assurance that they will produce what they are meant to produce, and need not prove too much to anyone.

By their indifference to fame and fortune; by their cheerful insistence that man and not his world needs changing; by their need for solitude as much as for company.

By their courage and by their patient endurance; by their passion for beauty and their toleration of ugliness; by their knowledge that jealousy and love are contradictions; by their sheer greatness.

These are the people who are "in the world but not of it." These are the "salt of the earth," who keep the whole earth from rotting. These are the ones who have learned to see infinity in a grain of sand and eternity in an hour.

These, to me, are the most profound words in all modern poetry:

"To see a World in a Grain of Sand,
And a Heaven in a Wild Flower,
Hold Infinity in the palm of your hand,
And Eternity in an hour." [4]

The poet who wrote those words knew what Christ meant by "eternal life." That is what you would see if you entered God's Kingdom: infinity in a grain of sand and eternity in an hour.

You would see, if you entered God's Kingdom – you will see when you enter God's Kingdom – that eternal

[4] William Blake, Auguries of Innocence.

life is not just endless time in which to live as you live now. Eternal life is a way of living. It is the way God lives. And those who live in eternal life, live with God. And of course they live forever! If a man lives with God, what should he do but live forever?[5]

And don't you see: if eternal life is a way of living, you can begin living it at any time. For you, then, every raindrop will be a little universe, as full of beauty and surprise as the whole earth. And a minute may teach you the meaning of time, which is, that all time is motion, toward or away from God.

To quote blessed Fra Giovanni[6]:

"There is nothing I can give you which you have not; but there is much you can take.

"No heaven can come to us unless our hearts find rest in it today – Take heaven.

"No peace lies hidden in the future which is not hidden in the present – Take peace.

"The gloom of the world is but a shadow; behind it, yet within our reach, is joy – Take joy."

Christ hangs on the cross, showing men how to die as he has shown them how to live. The two everlasting kinds of men hang on either side of him: the man who has been made bitter by the pain of life, and the man whose eyes have been opened by the pain of life. And the man whose eyes have been opened sees that to be with God is Paradise – even on the cross.

---

[5]John Donne, **Holy Sonnet VII.**
". . . You whose eyes
Shall behold God, and never tast deaths woe." (sic)

[6]A monk of the high Middle Ages.

The Third Word

The first word was for the sinner. The second was to the penitent.

The third word, to which we come now, was spoken to saints. Jesus says to the Virgin Mary, "Woman, behold thy son;" and to St. John, "Son, behold thy mother."

Christ is giving his mother into his friend's care: Mary, whom God chose to bear His son, and John, "the disciple whom Jesus loved." These are saints among the saints!

I cannot, of course, speak to you of sanctity as one who knows. I know only a little of what the saints tell us about themselves. I can only point, and say, "Out there – somewhere – out there is another kind of human life entirely, the life of Paradise before death, the life of the saint."

For the saint does not see just what we see, that I know. The saint sees reality, not the mere surface of it. You and I see the light of the sun striking off the surface of things. But the saint sees the light and the life of God pouring up out of the heart of things. It is because he sees through the surface of things into reality that the saint sees God. For God is Ultimate Reality. God is at the heart of everything.

Every normal man has five senses; and we suppose that every man sees the same world. But have you never thought how pathetically dependent our world is upon our way of looking at it?

Dogs, for example, see no color, but only various shades of grey; they do not see our world. If now God should add still another power to our eyes – beyond color – what would our world be then? It might become the world in which the saints live.

For God has given the saints special power. That is what saints are for: to show forth in this world the reality and power and love of God. The saints are the only perfect proof of God; for when we look at them we say, "Such a life cannot be explained except by power from on high."

But we do not really understand the saints, because they are the first members of a new race. Henceforth, the evolution of mankind is not physical any more, but spiritual.[7]

We have come up now from savagery to barbarism to civilization, and we stand on the brink of a new world once again. Savagery ends with the smelting of iron ore. Barbarism ends with the invention of the phonetic alphabet. Civilization is not yet even well begun; for civilization requires a spiritual man – a man, that is, who can see and obey God. And the saints are the first members of this spiritual race, as far advanced beyond us as we are advanced beyond mindless brutes.

Just as the first developed mind was something new on earth when it appeared, and opened up for its possessor a whole new universe and a whole new life, so these few developed and perfected spirits are something new on earth, and have entered into a life which we cannot even imagine. They are the descendants of Christ, who was a million years ahead of his time, and whose children are spiritual.

---

[7] Pierre Lecomte du Nouy, **Human Destiny**.

We can no better understand the world of a saint than a dog can understand music. We are like that blind man whose friends tried to explain the color scarlet to him; and at last he said, "I think it must be something like the sound of a trumpet." We grasp the beauty of the thing, but not the thing itself. To a great degree, these men who see things we cannot see and do things we cannot do, must always remain friendly foreigners to us.

Here, for example, is the 55th Verse of the 7th Chapter of the Book of Acts – beautiful to us – and very strange:

"Stephen, being full of the Holy Ghost, looked up steadfastly into heaven, and saw the glory of God, and Jesus standing on the right hand of God, and said, Behold, I see the heavens opened, and the Son of Man standing on the right hand of God."

It is by no means necessary to go to the saints of the Church to find a world different from ours. Look at the life of that odd genius and saint of innocence, the poet William Blake. I quote from Gilchrist, Blake's great biographer:

"On Peckham Rye it is, as he will in after years relate, that while quite a child, of eight or ten perhaps, he has his first vision. Sauntering along, the boy looks up and sees a tree filled with angels, bright angelic wings bespangling every bough like stars. Returning home, he relates the incident, and only through his mother's intercession escapes a thrashing from his honest father for telling a lie.

"Another time, one summer morn, he sees the haymakers at work, and amid them angelic figures walking.

"Blake had visits from the spiritual world in later years, in which the grown man believed as unaffectedly as ever had the boy of ten.

"One day, a traveler was telling bright wonders of some foreign city. 'Do you call that splendid?' broke in young Blake. 'I should call a city splendid in which the houses were of gold, the pavement of silver, and the gates ornamented with precious stones.' "

It is quite obvious to any reader of the Bible what heavenly city Blake had seen in vision. And it is quite foolish to attempt to dispose of this whole matter by saying that William Blake was mad. For if he was mad, so were all the prophets. As so was Marconi. And so was Gandhi. And so was Ramakrishna. And so was Christ. And so is every man who can see further than his contemporaries.

Are not these things there? They are there for the saints! I think that only death can show us what they see in life.

Think what an all-surrounding, all-encompassing "other" world the Bible takes for granted, that numinous, mysterious, yet most real world from which Christ came, and to which he returned, and which he never quite left.

Do you remember reading of the evening that Jesus walked on the water?

"Jesus constrained his disciples to get into the boat, and to go ahead of him to the other side of the lake, while he sent the multitudes away. And when he had sent the multitudes away, he went up into a mountain apart to pray. And when evening had come, he was there alone.

"But the boat was now in the midst of the lake, tossed by waves; for the wind was contrary. And in the fourth watch of the night Jesus went unto them, walking on the water . . . . !"

Where had he been, that he came walking thus on the water, lifted above the world?

And in the Garden of Gethsemane, the disciples came and found him "talking with the Father." Not praying blind as we pray, but talking with his Father. Who knows how many times he talked face to face with his Father, times when nobody came to find him doing it?

And at the Transfiguration on the Mount, what did Jesus do but walk out of this transitory life into the Eternal World, so that he appeared to his watching disciples as he is in eternity? His clothing, they said, became "exceeding white and glistening, such as no cleaner on earth could make it." No cleaner on earth. No.

I am trying to express what my mind cannot define, but what my heart knows to be true: There is a world within our world, a world we somehow do not see, in which the saints live with Christ. It is the Eternal World, the unchanging world, the world of God.

We live in it, too, but without seeing it. It is because we see only the surface of things and not the eternal heart of things that we are afraid and unhappy and unkind. And the great object of all our living must be, to keep praying and searching for this Kingdom of God, because it is the real home of every one of us.

Perhaps there is someone here to whom God will show the Eternal World in this life. I cannot tell, for God chooses His saints as He pleases.

But this I can tell you surely: on the day which you take to be the hardest day of your life, on the day of your death, that day your eyes will be opened. That day, if you have loved God and others, you will see pure beauty and know pure joy for the first time. That day you will enter the Eternal World.

C. S. Lewis has described the entrance into the Eternal World better than anyone else I know. What I reproduce here will already be familiar to many of you. It is part of a letter written by Screwtape, one of the Major Devils, to a Junior Tempter by the name of Wormwood. Little Wormwood had been given the assignment of bringing a certain man to hell; but now that man has died in the Christian Faith during an air raid, and gone to Eternal Life. The letter[8] follows:

"You have let a soul slip through your fingers . . . It makes me mad to think of it.

"How well I know what happened at the instant when they snatched him from you! There was a sudden clearing of his eyes (was there not?) as he saw you for the first time, and recognised the part you had had in him and knew that you had it no longer.

"Just think (and let it be the beginning of your agony) what he felt at that moment; as if a scab had fallen from an old sore, as if he were emerging from a hideous, shell-like tetter, as if he shuffled off for good and all a defiled, wet, clinging garment. By Hell, it is misery enough to see them in their mortal days taking off dirtied and uncomfortable clothes and splashing in hot water and giving little grunts of pleasure – stretching

[8]C. S. Lewis, **The Screwtape Letters** (1943).

their eased limbs. What, then, of this final stripping, this complete cleansing!

"The more one thinks about it, the worse it becomes. He got through so easily! No gradual misgivings, no doctor's sentence, no nursing home, . . . sheer, instantaneous liberation. One moment it seemed to be all our world; the feet burning with weariness, the heart cold with horrors, the brain reeling, the legs aching; next moment all this was gone, gone like a bad dream, never again to be of any account . . .

"Did you mark how naturally – as if he'd been born for it – the earth-born vermin entered the new life? How all his doubts became, in the twinkling of an eye, ridiculous? I know what the creature was saying to itself! 'Yes. Of course. It always was like this . . . You die and die, and then you are beyond death. How could I ever have doubted it?'

"As he saw you, he also saw Them. I know how it was. You reeled back dizzy and blinded . . . The degradation of it! – that this thing of earth and slime could stand upright and converse with spirits before whom you, a spirit, could only cower. Perhaps you had hoped that the awe and strangeness of it would dash his joy. But that is the cursed thing; the gods are strange to mortal eyes, and yet they are not strange. He had no faintest conception till that very hour of how they would look, and even doubted their existence. But when he saw them he knew that he had always known them and realised what part each one of them had played at many an hour in his life when he had supposed himself alone, so that now he could say to them, one by one, not, 'Who *are* you?' but 'So it was *you* all the time.' The dim consciousness of friends about him which had haunted his solitudes from infancy was now at last explained . . .

"He saw not only Them; he saw Him. This animal . . . could look on Him. What is blinding, suffocating fire to you, is now cool light to him, is clarity itself . . . ."

The Fourth Word

As the first three words from the cross are addressed to the three spiritual classes of men (sinners, penitents and saints), so now the next three are addressed to all men whatsoever, and decree a common destiny for us all. To all men Jesus speaks now of what must come to all – just because they are men.

"My God, my God, why has thou forsaken me?" – All men are lonely.

"I thirst." – All men feel pain.

"It is finished." – God alone can finish anything perfectly: all men experience frustration.

"My God, my God, why has thou forsaken me?"

Here – in the wonderful words of Martin Luther – "here God makes Himself very small in Christ." Here is the final sorrow for Christ, a sorrow he does not and cannot go beyond: he feels that he is forsaken by God.

We do not really know what it is to feel forsaken by God as Christ knew it. But we hint at what Christ felt, just the same. For our final comment upon any dismal scene is that it is "Godforsaken."

But plain loneliness, the state of being forsaken by men – we know what that is. It is the nearest we come to the pain which Christ felt, as man is often the nearest we come to God.

Loneliness, truly, is very close to God-forsakenness, even for Christ. For you will notice that Jesus is forsaken by man before he feels forsaken by God. He has been nailed to the cross by man, and spit upon by man, and mocked by man, and left to his fate by man a long, long time before he feels that God, too, has forsaken him.

And that is how loneliness comes to all men. That is how God-forsakenness comes when it comes. Our brothers turn against us; and at this horrid sight, God hides His face – and so is hidden from us. It is not many hours after our brothers forsake us that we feel God has gone away, too.

It is only the depths of Christ's deprivation we cannot share. Plain loneliness, that we share!

Indeed, I wonder if you can even imagine how much loneliness sits brooding in the houses of this town. I wonder if anyone can know this as a minister knows it. Will you believe me if I tell you that one of my principal duties is nothing more than to bring plain human company to those who are without it?

And why are so many wonderful people without human company? I will tell you exactly why, though the telling is a horrid matter. They are forsaken and forgotten, in most cases, because nobody can get anything more out of them!

Go and see for yourselves. Are the rich and influential ever left alone? Never. People crowd around them like bees around honey – and for the same reason. But the poor and the unimportant sit alone.

And let me ask you this question: Why is it only my business to bring company and humanity to the lonely? Why is it not your business, too?

You say you are too busy? This is correct. If you are too busy to be a human being, you are far too busy.

Nathaniel Hawthorne once wrote a story which he called "The Minister's Black Veil."

The minister in a small town one day appeared before his people wearing over his face a thick black veil. And when they said to him, "What are you doing?" – when they commanded him, "Take off that abominable thing!" – he answered, "You are all veiling your faces from one another. The day you drop your veils, that day I will take off mine."

Here is the first cause of human loneliness: the veiling of our faces from each other, the masking of our eyes, the hardening of our hearts – so that when some other heart seeks company, he cannot get in.

And who veils his face, who masks his eyes, who hardens his heart but a robber, who seeks to steal from his brother without being recognized? That is what we are – robbers! We seek to take the human company of our brother and to give him nothing in return. He tries to do the same to us.

The world is like the Italian theatre called "Commedia dell' Arte", in which all the players are masked. We go about with our masks clamped firmly on our faces, trying to guess what lies beneath the mask our neighbor wears.

You are afraid to take off your mask! You think nobody would like you if he saw you as you are. And all the time that is exactly what everybody who knows you desires most: to see you as God and time have made you; to see you as you really are; to see in you all the good and evil and joy and pain that he feels in himself.

That is what everyone desires: to finish with loneliness, the loneliness of being the only man in the world.

The veils we wear represent man's inhumanity to man; and man's inhumanity to man literally understood. No man on earth will admit to another that he is human!

The veils we wear have done terrible things to the human world. Do you remember Robert Burns' poem, "To a Field Mouse"? Burns was plowing and turned up the winter den of a field mouse. The mouse ran wickering away; and Burns called after him:

"I'm truly sorry Man's dominion
Has broken Nature's social union,
An' justifies th' ill opinion
Which makes thee startle."

Well said. The animals have been afraid of us for a long time. But now it is not merely "Nature's social union" we have broken, it is human society itself!

We have gone far beyond loneliness for each other: we live in mortal terror of each other. Nine-tenths of all the people who come to me in trouble are dreadfully afraid. And what are they afraid of? They are afraid of what other men may do to them.

Society is no longer society. It is a contest! It is war with limited weapons. I carry an insurance policy to defend me from any neighbor who may trip over my children's toys on my own front lawn – and sue me for ten thousand dollars. I am not simply deprived of my neighbor. I am afraid of him.

Here is man's vaunted dominion for you! Broken Nature's social union? Annihilated all human society whatever, I should say. To war against the animals, that was apparently necessary. But to war against your neighbor, to hide behind a veil, that is the death of man himself. (Much so-called "modern art" and "modern music" must surely be a sadistic and hysterical celebration of this death.) And each man must live and die in loneliness as the price for not loving his neighbor.

Now I am issuing a call for a few blessed fools – for a few blessed fools who are ready to take a risk for the love of God and man.

"Grace it is, and charity,
Crazed for Jesus Christ to be;
Who hath never been a fool,
Wisdom's scholar cannot be."

Those lines were written by Iacapone da Todi, one of the Italian mystics; and they are true lines. It is a sign of God's help and love – it is grace and charity – when anyone loves Christ enough to obey *him* instead of the sad and foolish conventions of the world.

And although the world will perhaps call you a fool if you take off your mask and appear to other men as you are, yet nobody will ever be really wise who is not willing to become a fool for Christ's sake – and the sake of other men. For as long as we wear masks, we learn nothing of the human heart. So long as you wear your mask, your brother will wear his. And although you may think you know all about him, you know nothing about him but what he chooses to show you. And though you may think you have many friends, you have no friends, but only a lot of actors whose names you know. And though you think you have much company, you are lonely enough to die of it.

Why is it wise and loving to act like a fool for Christ's sake? Because it *works*, like the rest of Christ's Way.

Because the minute you take off your mask, you stop being lonely. Because the minute you stop being a pretender, you become a loving invader of other men's hearts, bringing them what they need most. And what they need most is *you*.

I am therefore, as I said, issuing a call for a few blessed fools, for a few people who are ready, now that everything else has failed, to try the Way of Christ. Let us take off our masks and appear to our neighbors as we are. You will find that, very soon, your neighbor, with a sign of relief, will stop pretending, too. And the love of God will begin to appear once more in human society.

How happy for us if someday we shall understand: The love of God is not something we have or have not, just as we choose. The love of God in the human heart is the source of all man's other loves. Unless you are willing to become as simple and unpretending as Christ, you pervert your humanity. You end by putting your humanity to death. And to put this to death means that there is nothing left for you yourself to do but to die of loneliness.

How happy for us if someday we shall feel what we have lost through our pretending, and cry out, "My God, my God, come back! Why did I ever forsake You?"

The Fifth Word

The fifth word which Christ speaks from the cross is just "I thirst," and by it Christ means that he suffers pain in the body as all men must. You may well hear him say further, "And *you* thirst; all men whatsoever shall have pain," as once he said, "In the world you have tribulation."

There is no escape. Man, God's masterpiece, the one who is made in God's image, must suffer. The more a man is a man, the more he suffers, often enough. The mark of the spirit is that it collides with the world, and is wounded. We who have nerves that carry our thought out into the world must also have nerves that carry the outrages of the world back into the mind, to give us pain. In a word, the mark of rank in Nature is the ability to suffer.

Lobsters, I imagine, feel little pain – and equally little joy. And I have seen sharks, disemboweled on the deck of a fishing boat, eat their own livers.

But if you are so made that you can fall in love, if you are so made that a sunset is a kind of banquet to you, then you must be able to feel the world with an exquisite sensitivity. And that means you will also have pain.

There is no escape, not even in godliness. If the Son of God, the sinless one, must suffer so on his cross, how can we hope to escape pain through goodness?

It is strange how instinctively we feel in our hearts that our pain is a punishment for our sins. We feel this way because we know that we *deserve* punishment. We all feel guilty, more or less. And when we are in pain, we think, "This is God taking vengeance on me."

But it is not so. I am always telling somebody, "No, no; it is not necessarily what you did that brought this suffering upon you. Look at Christ. What wrong did *he* do? And yet he suffered most of all. God tries us all sore, good and bad alike."

And the person I am reassuring looks at me half in hope and half in doubt. He still believes in his heart that

God is taking vengeance on him. It would be so much easier to understand if God did, in fact, reward us exactly for our deeds in this life.

I can remember that when I was a child the surgeons came one night to operate on me in my bed at home. But I had had all the surgery I could stand. And when they clamped the ether cone over my face, I cried out, "I'll be good! I'll be good!" – as if I knew this terrible night had come of stealing cookies, as if it could not happen to good children.

But it is not so. You would not escape agony though you became one of the saints in the calendar. God knows *they* had pain enough: St. Paul with his malaria, St. Stephen stoned to death, St. Peter crucified upside-down, St. Ignatius holding out his poor leg to be broken once again, and saying, "It must be endured."

Some still think as the Old Testament Jews thought. When you are in pain, someone may say, as Job's friends said to him, "This is the portion of a wicked man from God."

But Job knew it was not so. And it is not so. God can punish more mercifully and more constructively than *this*. God does not need to burn people on stove lids or trip them off ladders. He has all eternity. And suffering which comes directly from *Him* is for *correction*.

Once the Jews pointed out a blind man to Jesus and asked, "Who sinned, this man or his parents, that he is blind?" And Jesus answered. "This man sinned not, neither his parents; but he is blind so that the work of God may be done in him."

I will give this, without a blush, all the force that is in it. What is Jesus saying here but that a man is blind because that is part of God's plan? God plans to bring out of this blindness something glorious.

In this case, the glorious result was that Christ healed the blind man so that he saw. In Milton's case, the glorious result was such poetry as the world has seldom heard. In some cases, the glorious result is hidden from us. But every Christian bears his pain in the certain knowledge that God will bring out of it something glorious. For the greatest single proof of God's power is that He is able to bring good even out of evil.

This is what I think of suffering. I believe what Christ clearly tells me. Surely, since pain is here, it is here by God's permission. And if God permits it, He permits it because it is a necessary part of His plan. I do not say that He directly wills or desires it. But He *permits* it, because its final results *can* be good. Pain *can* issue in glory, God's glory and ours.

"For," writes St. Paul, "I reckon that the sufferings of this present time are not worthy to be compared with the glory which shall be revealed in us." And I suspect, though the Apostle does not say so, that the glory would not come without the pain. For light can be seen only against darkness; and goodness is beautiful because we are accustomed to wickedness; and not even the loveliest things in all this world are lovely to the man who has never suffered.

And now I have said (which may be too much for some of you) that pain is necessary to the development of the kind of people God desires, and that He will bring good even out of the apparent evil of suffering.

Please do not tell me that pain is all the devil's fault; for not even the devil can walk the earth without

God's permission. And please do not tell me that pain is all man's fault; for how is man to blame for earthquakes and volcanic eruptions and the mortal bite of the cobra?

Believe me, there is nothing for a Christian to do but to say, "When God made this world, He said that it was good. Who am I to say that it is evil? Weeping may endure for a night; but joy cometh in the morning. Though I may suffer a while, yet I know that I am an eternal creature. And I know that the good God would not require this suffering of me were it not for my own eternal good. I will praise God for whatever He sends. 'Though God *slay* me, yet will I trust in Him'."[9]

Is it impossible for you to trust God this far? Is it impossible for you to see that, as the caterpillar must go through the dark of the cocoon to grow his wings, so a man must go through the dark of pain to grow his? Is it impossible for you to see that, as the lobster must shatter his shell time after time and make it again to become a lobster, so a man must break his heart time after time and find it again to become a man? Is it impossible for you to see that what looks evil from the temporal point of view may be good from the eternal point of view? Is it impossible for you to see that what is hard on the body may give life to the soul? Is it impossible for you to see that those who do not experience and recognize these things do not really live, but only exist?

If all this is impossible for you, then perhaps you will try to escape by pretending that pain is an illusion. Those who cannot trust God very often pretend that pain is an

---

[9] Job.

illusion. They feel they must protect God's good reputation. And they do not love God enough to swallow any of His nasty medicine. And so they say that pain is an illusion.

But you will not escape *that* way, either. For if pain is an illusion, it is an exceedingly *painful* illusion, isn't it?

"There was a faith healer of Deal
Who said, Although pain isn't real,
When I sit on a pin
And it punctures my skin,
I dislike what I fancy I feel."

That silly little limerick may seem a bit undignified, but it makes the point well. Would those who claim that pain is an illusion stand in the way of a stampeding herd of cattle? Should anybody be so foolish as to philosophize that pain is merely a construction of the mind, or an exception in God's scheme of things?

The sooner we accept pain as a reality, the sooner we will learn how to deal with it. For nothing in this world conforms itself to our desires, but only to God's desires. Growing up consists to a large extent simply of accepting the world as God has made it. And the mark of babies of all ages is, that they require the world to be some other way. A religious man is one who loves and trusts the Maker of all things enough to like the way that He has made them.

You may convince yourself, evidently (at least, some people can), that pain does not exist. But then you are not painless; you are only deluded.

And what is far worse, you have sought to escape from the kind of life which Jesus Christ holds out to you from the cross. For Christ on the cross is not showing you a way to *escape* from pain, but a way to bear it and to bring great things out of it. And if, indeed, pain is not a part of God's world but only a human illusion, then why did Christ groan on the cross, and why did he say so plaintively, so humanly, "I thirst"?

Books without number have been written on the problem of pain, some good, some bad. But what interests me is the fact that Jesus never once in all his life treated pain as a *problem*!

To the mind of Christ, God is *finally* responsible for *everything.* Jesus sees God, therefore, as permitting pain, too. If there is any problem, it is only the problem of bringing the heart to obedience and trust in God.

This is truest and best. God *is* ultimately responsible, be there other persons and other wills without number. God created this world; and therefore He must finally answer for what happens in it. And Jesus has no more than this to say about pain: "Receive this, too, at God's hand." He agrees with Job, who said long before him, "What! Shall we receive good from God, and not evil?"

Pain, I fully believe, must be the mother of eternal pleasure. I feel certain we shall discover, on the other side, that our few hours of pain have purchased us endless joy. The soul appears to be born into eternity through the sufferings of the body. And pain seems everywhere to create a capacity for pleasure. Indeed, pleasure intense enough is hard to *distinguish* from pain. I wonder if any man who had never felt real pain could *endure* the Vision of God.

The Sixth Word

Christ says on the cross, "It is finished."

This does not mean, "My suffering is finished." It does not mean, "My hard life is finished." Above all, Christ does not mean, "*I* am finished: I have failed."

No. Christ means, "It is *perfectly* finished." This is Christ's announcement to all men for all time that the work of Christ on earth is complete. Here is the finish of a perfect life, a perfect work, a perfect victory.

Soon now, even the cross itself will be unburdened. It will be no longer a crucifix burdened with a suffering body. It will become that bare cross that stands above our altars to show that Christ is resurrected and triumphant. Jesus has redeemed even the wood of his cross.

"It is finished."

Only Christ can say this. No man finishes anything perfectly.

[10] There is a strange and wonderful contrast between our lives and the life of Christ in this respect. We succeed at the little things we do. We have hours, even days, crowned with success. In many particular objects of his life, a man succeeds. And yet, of his whole life taken together, he must say, "It is not finished." No matter how well any man may appear to succeed, he is always dissatisfied at heart. Our lives are forever incomplete, unfinished, disappointing.

But the Lord Jesus failed in everything he did – except the sum of all he did. Each separate hour of his life is

---

[10] This section follows William James, the great 19th century American philosopher and psychologist whose interest in religion, like that of Jung, was very great.

a failure. Yet his whole life is a success. After the most tragic life the world has ever seen, he alone can say, "It is finished."

I may seem to be speaking to you about something remote, about something which does not really matter, because I am telling you what Jesus Christ said on his cross two thousand years ago. But Jesus is not really remote from you at all.

And he is not speaking these words from his cross merely to a crowd of Jews and Romans now long dead. He is speaking these words to *you*.

And he is not dying to save just that handful of people who stand around his cross back there on Golgotha outside the ancient city of Jerusalem. Christ died to save *you*.

Christ died for *you*.

How many hundreds of times you may have heard that, I can only guess. And how little or how much it means to you, I can only guess.

But I do not have to guess what God *intends* it to mean to you. God intends that it shall mean all the difference between despair and joy. For what Christ died to save us from was *death*. And I do not mean the death of this body (we must all pass through that). I mean *eternal death*, the death of the soul.

The only thing which can finally kill the soul is despair. And the only one who can save us from despair is Christ. All men feel incomplete, unfinished. And it is Christ alone who can complete them.

When I say that Christ died to save you, I do not mean anything vague or impractical. I mean, he died to save you in your innermost feelings from a world where everybody gets hurt, and where some get hurt beyond repair. I mean, he died to save you from the sorrows and disappointments of your own life.

He says, in effect, "If you make me your Lord, then you become my soldier; and you enter into my victory over the world – so that, though the world will wound you, it cannot make you despair. If you are in me, and I in you, nothing can finally shut you out from joy in God."

This is the very heart of the Christian victory over life.

You *need* to know that Christ has triumphed over the world. You *need* to wrap up your life with his. You need to know that, as his soldier, you can share his victory. You need to know these things because, if you are like the rest of mankind, you are going to feel like an utter failure, yourself.

Take the happiest man, the man most envied by the world; and nine times out of ten his innermost feeling is one of failure. We are all quite certain that, if only we were rich and famous, we would feel successful – and we are all quite wrong in thinking so.

The German poet, Goethe, was the most celebrated genius of his time. He was one of those rare men to whom God seems to give everything. He was brilliant beyond belief, and just as handsome as he was brilliant. He had robust health and enormous personal magnetism. Men spoke of him as of a demigod. Everyone was fascinated by him; everyone sought his company; his work was invariably applauded to the skies. Yet hear what he has to say, at last, about his own life:

"I will say nothing," he writes, "against the course of my existence. But at bottom it has been nothing but pain and burden . . . . It is but the perpetual rolling of a rock that must be raised again forever."[11]

When such a giant as Goethe can express himself this way, how must it be with lesser men?

Again, what man, single-handed, was ever on the whole as successful as Martin Luther? He was the very Morning Star of the Protestant Reformation, and lived to see his best-loved ideals become the religious practice of men. Yet when he had grown old, he looked back upon his life as if it had been an absolute failure. Hear him:

"I am utterly weary of life. I pray the Lord will come forthwith and carry me hence. Let Him come, above all, with His Last Judgment. I will stretch out my neck, the thunder will burst forth, and I shall be at rest."

And having a necklace of white agates in his hand at this time, he added, "O God, grant that it may come without delay. I would readily eat up this necklace today, for the Judgment to come tomorrow."

A noble lady, one day when Luther was dining with her, said to him, "Doctor, I wish you may live forty years to come."

"Madam," he replied, "rather than live forty years more, I would give up my chance of Paradise."

Failure, then – failure!

It may be that you have no conscious sense of failure. I observe, nevertheless, what goes on in your life. You are always trying to fill your life up. I know. I do the

---

[11] This and the comment on Luther which follows in substance from William James, **The Varieties of Religious Experience.**

same thing. There is a quality almost of hysteria in the frenzy with which most of us strive to fill our hours with activity.

We give all sorts of good reasons for our hectic running to and fro. But the real reason is that if we sat still for a moment, God would tell us we are succeeding at the wrong things.

God sent us here, not to impress our neighbors but to help our neighbors. God sent us here, not to take things but to give things. God sent us here, not to get into *Who's Who*, but to get into heaven. God sent us here to become, not first of all good businessmen or housewives or doctors or plumbers – or even ministers, but to become *good human beings*!

To become a good human being, that would be to imitate Christ, and that would be success! But we choose, instead, to succeed at something easier. Therefore we are all failures.

We fill up our lives in different ways; but the emptiness is the same: it is the feeling of human failure in us all. And God has had pity on our failings. He has sent Christ to complete us.

Listen, then, to the sixth word from the cross:

Christ says, "It is finished." And by this he means that he has won victory, not only for himself but for all who love and follow him.

The Seventh Word

"And when Jesus had cried with a loud voice, he said, Father, into thy hands I commend my spirit; and having said thus, he gave up the ghost."

Here is the seventh and final word from the cross, the last words ever spoken by our Lord in this life. And these words accompany what was, in our Lord's case, *strictly speaking*, the *act* of dying.

Notice what the Bible *says* about his dying. The Bible records that he said, "Father, into thy hands I *commend* my spirit," and, that having said this, he *gave up* his spirit.

His dying was not entirely like our dying; for he is God as well as man. He does not "feel the approach of death" as men feel it. He is not "carried off" as men are. His death, like his coming down into our world in the first place, was his *own act*, something done willingly for love of men.

In the 17th Verse of the 10th Chapter of St. John's Gospel, Jesus says, "Therefore doth my Father love me, because I lay down my life . . . *No man taketh it from me*, but I lay it down of myself. I have power to lay it down, and I have power to take it again."

And he *did* lay it down; and he *did* take it again – on Easter Day!

"Into thy hands I commend my spirit."

Christ here begins to return to his Father out of the flesh. "The Word was made flesh and dwelt among us," St. John says. That is the King James Version of Scripture.

But St. John really said it far more beautifully in his own language: he said that God came and "tented" among us in Christ's flesh, as strangers in the East may come and pitch their tents overnight.

And now, as he commends his spirit into the Father's hands, Jesus begins to fold that tent of flesh which has covered him on earth. He will be buried in its torn folds on Good Friday – and be resurrected in a glorified body on Easter Day – and upon Ascension Day return fully to his Father.

But consider what he takes with him when he returns fully to his Father. Think what a foothold we have in the very heart of God! For Christ did not take our human nature *temporarily*: he took our human nature *forever.* He not only *was* both God and man on *earth*: he still is both God and man in *heaven*.

He did not slough off his humanity when he ascended again into heaven. *He took his human nature with him.* He carried human nature up into the nature of God, so that these two natures which were once combined in Christ on earth are now combined in God in heaven.

This is a truth which I do not believe most Christians either know or understand. We do not realize how greatly God has glorified mankind. For first Christ came and took human flesh and human nature; he became one of us. That alone honored our flesh and our nature forever.

But then, finally, Christ carried our nature with him up into the very Godhead. Now it can be said (and it is a thought almost dreadful in its majesty and in its demands upon us): *human nature*, the very same human nature which we vilify and distrust and abuse and cover with dirt upon earth – this human nature sits enthroned as part of God upon God's throne.

Surely I must be right in thinking we do not understand these things. For if we understood these things, how could we live as we do?

No man who steadily held before his eyes the vision of Christ clothing himself with human flesh could willingly soil his body, the same body that Christ glorified, with the dirty sins of the flesh. And no man who really understood that his human nature sits enthroned in heaven would willingly corrupt his nature, the same nature which Christ now glorifies, with the even dirtier sins of the spirit.

Least of all could we go on year after year treating the bodies and souls of other people as we do. For every fragment of human flesh which suffers on this globe is the blood brother of that flesh which suffered on the cross. And every human personality torn and corrupted by the evils and injustices of human society is the spiritual brother of the human personality which Christ now possesses in heaven.

I mean some very concrete and real things by these seemingly broad and general statements. I am not talking out of a love for beautiful visions, but out of a love for good human behavior. When I speak to you about the human flesh and human nature of Christ, I am speaking to you about what Christ, by his example, commands us to do with *our* flesh and *our* nature.

I mean, for example, that no Christian husband is permitted to live selfishly with his wife (you know what I mean). He must look upon her with real love, and feel her happiness to be *his* happiness. Otherwise, he is no better than any adulterer – and *worse* than *some*!

For in the language which Christ teaches us, adultery is no longer purely a legal matter, but an attitude of the mind towards the flesh. What does Christ say? He does not say, "Whoever looks at a woman (except his wife) with nothing but lust, commits adultery." He says, "Whoever looks at any woman at all in that selfish way" – It may be a man's own wife!

I mean (to extend the principle) that no Christian is permitted to *use* any other person in the world as a tool, as a means to obtain anything, even the best things. People are not a *means* to anything. People are all *final objects in themselves*.

God did not put your brother here to make a pavement or a staircase for *you*. When God created your brother, he did not have *you* in mind at all: He had your brother in mind. If you think there is something final about you, you are right. But there is also something final about your brother.

There is something final about *everybody*. There is something final about *me*, little as I like to take the responsibility for it. In all time and in all space, there never has been and never will be again anybody just like me. My friends love to contemplate that fact, and my enemies detest that fact.

Nevertheless, I am unique. And, with all my faults, God loves me. "For He would not have created anything if He had not loved it." And God desires the kind of happiness which I alone, in all the universe, can give Him by my love for Him. For, you see, poor though my love for Him is, it is unlike the love of any other man. That is what is final about me. And that is what is final about *you*.

One last thing:

The Creator God has always known and understood us. And yet, it is one thing to *know* a creature and quite another thing to *be* that creature. It is one thing for God to know us, and another thing for God to *be* us. And now we have a God who has *been* us, a God who has *been a man.* Jesus has commended his spirit into the Father's hands.

Now, indeed, we have an Advocate, a *Pleader* with the Father, Jesus Christ the Righteous. And he is not merely Jesus Christ the Righteous – that is somewhat too stern. He is Jesus Christ the *Understanding* also – that is why he shall come to judge the earth. He knows the earth as one who has *lived* on earth. And he knows man as one born of woman.

"And he is the propitiation – the compensation – for our sins." There was no other good enough to pay the price for sin, and so Christ has done this. Christ has died for my sinfulness, so that now I, too, may commend my soul into God's hands and hope to see heaven.